CONTENTS

Bernhard Kutzler

Improving Mathematics Teaching with DERIVE

A Guide for Teachers

Translated from German into English by: Tim Boykett

 Chartwell-Bratt

 Studentlitteratur

British Library Cataloguing in Publication Data
A catalogue record for this book is available from the British Library

Typesetting: Bernhard Kutzler, Hagenburg
Printing and binding: Studentlitteratur, Lund

Many of the pictures were produced using Microsoft Powerpoint. Their use was explicitly authorised by Microsoft Deutschland GmbH.

Most software and hardware names mentioned in this book are registered trademarks.

© Bernhard Kutzler and Chartwell-Bratt 1996.

Chartwell-Bratt (Publishing and Training) Ltd
ISBN 0-86238-422-2

Printed in Sweden
Studentlitteratur, Lund
ISBN 91-44-00169-X

Printing/Year	1	2	3	4	5	6	7	8	9	10		2000	99	98	97	96

The newest generation of mathematical tools comprises computer programs called "Computer Algebra Systems". A computer algebra system is for formulae, what an ordinary calculator is for numbers. Just as one can enter two numbers into a calculator and add them with a single press of a button, so one can enter an expression into a computer algebra system and, with a single keypress, expand, differentiate, integrate, solve with respect to a variable or otherwise manipulate it. Most commercial computer algebra systems can, along with algebraic manipulations as indicated above, also calculate with numbers, plot graphs and are programmable. Thus they automate the most important mathematical skills. One of these all-round performers is DERIVE, developed by *Soft Warehouse, Inc.* (Honolulu, Hawaii).

On the basis of their widespread availability, even for the simplest of machines, computer algebra systems are probably the greatest challenge to mathematics teaching today: up to 80% of the problems laboriously learnt and exercised in schools today are solvable with DERIVE. New methods of mathematics teaching and learning appear: teachers and students can concentrate more on the solution of problems instead of laboriously training calculation skills. Even changes in teaching methodology are foreseeable.

Many mathematics teachers are insecure in the face of these developments, and understandably so: they have learnt to teach mathematics in a very particular way, and find themselves confronted with a tool, for which (almost) no-one can answer the question: "Wie nehma'n mir ihm denn?". (This rather extreme Austrian expression first needs translation into German: "Wie sollen wir es anpacken?" before we attempt to translate it into the English "How should we deal with this?". It originates with the Viennese actor Hans Moser, when he played a porter who had to carry a rather large and extremely heavy trunk from a house.) Hans Moser managed the trunk. And we will also manage to confront the challenge of computer algebra systems through our readiness to re-educate ourselves and renew our methods. The maxim, hammered into students today, that one must always be prepared to learn anew, to retrain on the job, applies also to mathematics teachers.

This book is an introduction to *teaching* with DERIVE. It is based upon DERIVE Version 3 and is directed at mathematics teachers from the 7th grade onwards, lecturers of introductory courses and students at teaching colleges. After a short presentation of DERIVE (Chapter 1), we show how this tool could be used in contemporary teaching (Chapter 2). This is followed by a perspective on the mathematics teaching of the future (Chapter 3). Examples for teaching (Chapter 4), Tips and Tricks (Chapter 5) and a description of the undocumented feature, user-defined menus (Chapter 6) make up the practical part of the book. Then comes a quick look behind the facade of a computer algebra system (Chapter 7). To finish we make a historical-philosophical examination of the implications of computer algebra technologies (Chapter 8).

Chapters 2,3,7 and 8 are predominately system independent and have value for users of other systems. Chapters 4,5 and 6 are system specific and presume that the reader can use DERIVE.

Those who seek an introduction to the *use* of DERIVE are advised to look at my easily read book *"Mathematics on the PC - Introduction to DERIVE"* (ISBN 3-9500364-1-5), intended for private study. The text leads the reader through many themes of mathematics, teaching the use of DERIVE and simultaneously introduces some of the ideas needed for teaching. The methods of working with the system are taught to a level needed for practical work in teaching or at home.

In this chapter we present DERIVE with the aid of many examples. In the process we will see how to input expressions, the commands we need to work with them, and the resultant screen displays. For those who have not yet worked with DERIVE, this chapter will act as an introduction to the system. Those already familiar with DERIVE will become familiar with our method for describing interactions with the system.

First let's look at the bottom four lines of the screen. Displayed there is the instruction menu and the current system information:

```
COMMAND: Author Build Calculus Declare Expand Factor Help Jump soLve Manage
         Options Plot Quit Remove Simplify Transfer Unremove moVe Window approX
Enter option
                                    Free:100%              Derive Algebra
```

One works with the system by activating commands, e.g. the ›Author‹ command serves to input an expression. Commands are activated by pressing the capital letter in the command word (in this case: ›A‹).

Our first example is the expansion of the polynomial $(2x + \frac{3}{4})^5$. First we input the polynomial using the ›Author‹ command:

❑   [A]uthor (2x+3/4)^5 [↵]

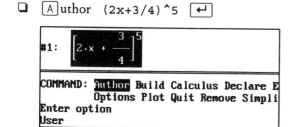

The computer displays the expression "two dimensionally", i.e. with the exponent raised and built-up fractions, then writes a label number (in this case #1) in front of it. We can later refer to this expression by this label. The expansion of the polynomial is performed with the ›Expand‹ command.

❏ $\boxed{\text{E}}$xpand

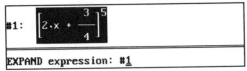

In the space where the menu is usually displayed, the expression to be expanded is requested (›EXPAND Expression:‹), with the (so far the only possible) expression #1 as default. By simply pressing the return key we accept this default.

❏ $\boxed{\leftarrow}$

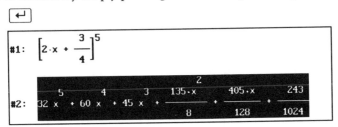

The result appears as the second expression on the screen, with the label number #2. It is marked and is the default expression for the next operation.

DERIVE can also work with variables. Not only that, but it makes use of fractions to guarantee exact answers. As our next example we will calculate the second differential of the expression $x^3 \sin(x) \cos(x)$.

❏ $\boxed{\text{A}}$uthor x^3sinxcosx $\boxed{\leftarrow}$

```
      3
#3:  x  SIN(x)·COS(x)
```

You see from this example how easy it is to input expressions into the system. Often we can simply forget the multiplication signs and the parentheses for the arguments to sine and cosine functions. To differentiate, we must invoke the ›Calculus‹ sub-menu,

❏ $\boxed{\text{C}}$alculus

```
CALCULUS: Differentiate Integrate Limit Product Sum Taylor Vector
```

and once there we select the ›Differentiate‹ command.

❏ $\boxed{\text{D}}$ifferentiate

```
CALCULUS DIFFERENTIATE expression: #3
```

The information required to carry out this command will be requested by the system. First we enter the expression to be differentiated, where the previous (marked) expression is the default.

❏ [↵]

CALCULUS DIFFERENTIATE variable: x

Then we are prompted for the name of the differentiation variable, where the default can be accepted by pressing the return key.

❏ [↵]

CALCULUS DIFFERENTIATE: Order: 1

The computer defaults to the first derivative. Since we want the second derivative, we replace the default 1 with 2.

❏ 2 [↵]

$$\#4: \quad \left[\frac{d}{dx}\right]^2 (x^3 \cdot SIN(x) \cdot COS(x))$$

The resulting expression #4 is then simply expression #3 with the differential operator applied. To actually calculate the derivative, we use the ›Simplify‹ command.

❏ [S]implify [↵]

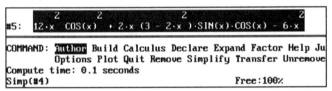

```
#5: 12·x² COS(x)² + 2·x (3 - 2·x² )·SIN(x)·COS(x) - 6·x²

COMMAND: Author Build Calculus Declare Expand Factor Help Ju
         Options Plot Quit Remove Simplify Transfer Unremove
Compute time: 0.1 seconds
Simp(#4)                                          Free:100%
```

Expression #5 is the second derivative of $x^3 \sin(x) \cos(x)$. The second last line shows the computation time (0.1 seconds). The annotation ›Simp(#4)‹ indicates the origin of the expression, in this case from the application of ›Simplify‹ to expression #4. These annotations exist for all expressions and can be freely modified by the user.

Next we calculate the indefinite integral of $x^3 \sin(x) \cos(x)$. For this we need to highlight expression #3 again. The highlight is moved with the arrow keys [↑] and [↓]. Press the up arrow key twice to highlight expression #3.

❏ [↑] [↑]

$$\#3: \quad x^3 \; SIN(x) \cdot COS(x)$$

Integrals are calculated using the ›Integrate‹ command in the ›Calculus‹ sub-menu.

❏ [C]alculus [I]ntegrate [↵]

```
CALCULUS INTEGRATE variable: x
```

The default integration variable x is accepted, and the prompt for the limits is ignored by simply pressing the enter key.

❏ [↵]

```
CALCULUS INTEGRATE: Lower limit: _              Upper limit:
```

[↵]

```
       ⌠ 3
#6:    ⎮ x ·SIN(x) COS(x) dx
       ⌡
```

The actual calculation is performed by simplifying the expression.

❏ [S]implify [↵]

So far, so good; a first impression of algebraic computation and interaction with the computer. Let's go on to some other aspects of DERIVE.

DERIVE can also carry out numerical calculations, doing much more than a traditional pocket calculator. For instance the only limit to the size of the numbers used is the memory available, a restriction that means almost nothing today.

❏ [A]uthor 23^45 [↵]

   [S]implify [↵]

```
          45
#8:   23

#9:   18956258430116202791319715713277227626159289499745290235663543
```

This number has 62 digits, but that is by no means the limit of what we can do. How many digits does the factorial of 567 have? Let's have a look.

❏ [A]uthor 567! [↵]

   [S]implify [↵]

```
#10: 567!

#11: 5494839840283956596617332956859015449349787508895279453048005749971967522255
```

In the standard font this result is about 1.8 metres long and reaches far over the right edge of the screen. To calculate the exact number of digits without counting them, we use the ›approX‹ command. While ›Simplify‹ gives exact results, ›approX‹ calculates a numerical approximation and prints it as a decimal.

❑   appro X   ↵

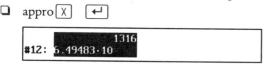

The use of scientific notation for numerical values is a major bonus for us. We can simply read from the screen that the number 567! has $1316+1 = 1317$ digits. The prime factorisation of this number can be calculated with the ›Factor‹ command.

❑   ↑   (to highlight expression #11)

   F actor   ↵

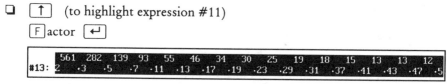

Here too, the answer reaches far over the edge of the screen. In such a case we can always shift the expression left and right with the Ctrl - → and Ctrl - ← keys.

An irrational number such as π remains unchanged by the ›Simplify‹ command. However the ›approX‹ command can be used to obtain a numerical approximation.

❑   A uthor pi   ↵

   appro X   ↵

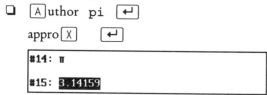

The default is a six-digit approximation. If one wants, for instance, a thousand digits of π, one either changes the default parameters, or uses the APPROX function which takes a second argument specifying the number of digits to calculate and display.

❑   A uthor approx(pi,1000)   ↵

   S implify   ↵

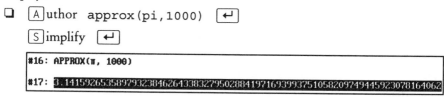

Many other commands are also available as functions, for example DIF to differentiate, INT to integrate, EXPAND to expand polynomials or FACTOR to factorise.

With DERIVE it is very simple to plot functions. To plot the graph of sin(*x*) we first enter the expression, then use the ›Plot‹ command to create a graphics window.

❏ 　Ａ uthor sinx 　⏎

　　Ｐ lot 　⏎

#18: SIN(x)

PLOT: Beside Under Overlay

The graphics window can be placed beside or below the algebra window, or even layered over it. It is often advantageous to lay it beside the algebra window, so we can keep both windows visible and usable.

❏ 　Ｂ eside 　⏎

PLOT BESIDE: At column: 40

The default is to split the screen in the middle, so that the algebra and graphics windows appear about the same size. Once we have accepted the default a graphics window is created and instead of the algebra menu a graphics menu is displayed. The graphics menu's ›Plot‹ command is used to plot the graph of the expression highlighted in the algebra window.

❏ 　⏎

　　Ｐ lot 　⏎

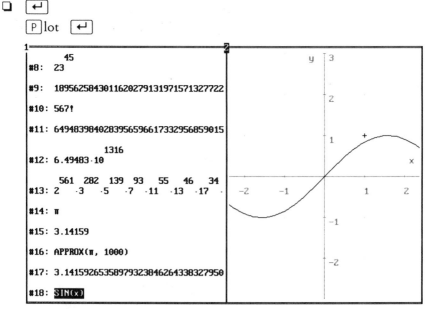

We can now move between the graphics and algebra windows. To move we use the ›Algebra‹ command in the graphics window and the ›Plot‹ command in the algebra window, or we can use the [F1] key. The currently active window can be recognised by the type of menu that is displayed, or by the marked window number in the upper left corner.

To see more of the sine curve we use the [F10] key as an abbreviation for the ›Zoom‹ command.

❑   [F10]

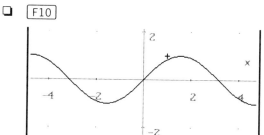

Now we add a plot of the corresponding Taylor polynomial. We switch to the algebra window, invoke the ›Calculus‹ sub-menu and select the ›Taylor‹ command.

❑   [A]lgebra   (to move into the algebra window)
    [C]alculus [T]aylor   ... answer all questions with [↵]
    [S]implify [↵]

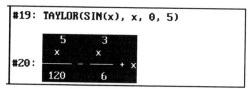

#19: TAYLOR(SIN(x), x, 0, 5)

$$\#20:\quad \frac{x^5}{120} - \frac{x^3}{6} + x$$

Expression #20 is the fifth order Taylor polynomial around the point $x = 0$. One plots the graph as follows:

❑   [P]lot   (to move into the graphics window)
    [P]lot   (to plot the highlighted expression)

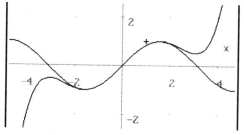

One can work interactively in the graphics window, in much the same way as one uses a graphics calculator. The graphics pointer, a cross, currently at position (1,1)

can be moved with the arrow keys. The current coordinates of the cross are displayed in the bottom left of the screen.

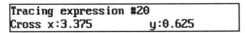

The trace mode, switchable with the ⌜F3⌝ key, is very useful. When on, the graphics pointer moves up or down at the same x-coordinate onto the most recently plotted graph. The cross becomes a box and moves only along the plotted graph.

❑   ⌜F3⌝

   Pressing ⌜→⌝ moves the graphics box to the right.

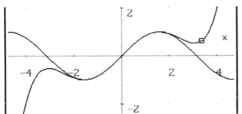

The coordinates of the box are displayed in the bottom left corner, with the number of the expression that generated the inspected graph displayed above:

```
Tracing expression #20
Cross x:3.375          y:0.625
```

With the ⌜↑⌝ and ⌜↓⌝ keys one can move between the graphs.

❑   ⌜↑⌝

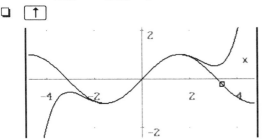

After changing to the sine curve the following appears in the lower left of the screen.

```
Tracing expression #18
Cross x:3.375          y:-0.2187
```

To investigate the area around the cross (or box, if we are in trace mode), we can change the range of the plot.

❑   R ange

The range can be specified either by explicitly entering the borders or by shifting the borders with the arrow keys (left picture). After pressing the enter key, the graph inside the new range will be plotted again (right picture).

❑   ↵

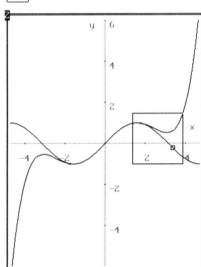 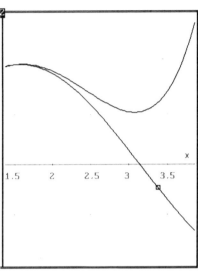

With DERIVE we can also plot 3-dimensional graphs of expressions in two variables.

❑   A lgebra   (to move into the algebra window)

    A uthor   x^4-y^4   ↵

    P lot   U nder   ↵   (to invoke a second graphics window)

    P lot   (to plot the highlighted expression)

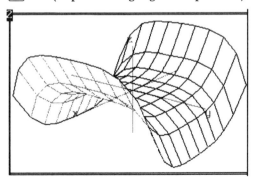

A wireframe model of the graph is generated. The quality of the graph and thus also the necessary compute time can be increased by lowering the mesh-size with the ›Grid‹ command.

❑ $\boxed{G}$ rid

GRIDS: x: <u>10</u>   y: <u>10</u>

The default is a mesh with 10 grid panels in each direction. To change to 20 panels, we use the tab key to move between the prompts.

❑   20 $\boxed{\rightleftarrows}$ 20 $\boxed{\leftarrow}$

$\boxed{P}$ lot

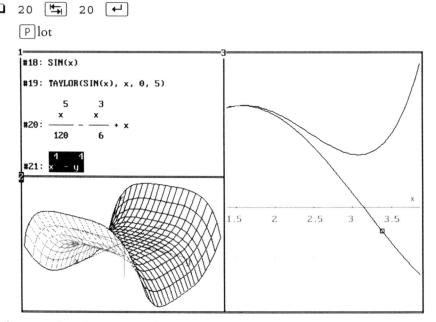

There are thus three types of window; algebra, 2D graphics and 3D graphics. They can be freely created and arranged with one another.

To finish, let's look at an example of programming in DERIVE. The built-in factorial function has already been seen. Let's define our own version with the name F. We use the IF function, which takes as first argument the condition to be tested, as second argument the result to return if the condition is fulfilled and as third argument the value to return in the case that the condition is not fulfilled. We use the following definition:

$$f(n):=\begin{cases} 1 & \text{if} \quad n=0 \\ n \cdot f(n-1) & \text{otherwise} \end{cases}$$

❑ $\boxed{\text{A}}$lgebra (to move into the algebra window)

$\boxed{\text{A}}$uthor f(n):=if(n=0,1,n f(n-1)) $\boxed{\leftarrow}$

#22: F(n) := IF(n = 0, 1, n·F(n − 1))

Now let's test our function F on the number 7, using a trailing equals sign to force an immediate simplification (i.e. direct application of the ›Simplify‹ command).

❑ $\boxed{\text{A}}$uthor f(7)= $\boxed{\leftarrow}$

#23: F(7) = 5040

The preceding examples from the fields of algebra, arithmetic, graphics and programming give an introduction to what is possible with DERIVE. Those who want to learn or know more about the system should consult my book "*Mathematics on the PC - Introduction to DERIVE*", mentioned in the introduction.

To finish off this chapter, we look at the question "Why DERIVE?". The following properties distinguish DERIVE from other similar systems, making it the best available system for school teaching:

• The simplicity of learning and using the system is vitally important, both for acceptance by average students and for teachers who have some kind of timidity regarding computers.

• The extremely low hardware demands (DERIVE runs on all PCs with at least 512 Kbytes memory, and works even without a hard drive or Windows) mean that the system can be recommended even to schools with older machines and/or limited budgets.

• In comparison with all similar systems, DERIVE is the most mathematically correct (some examples are to be found in the next chapter). Especially in the first contact with a subject, an excessively casual approach from the student or tools should not be expected or tolerated.

• DERIVE is the most economical of all systems. In view of the limited finances that most schools have for software purchases, this is an important factor.

CHAPTER 2

DERIVE IN TRADITIONAL MATHEMATICS TEACHING

Not much imagination is necessary to see that the teaching of mathematics could be radically altered by a tool such as DERIVE. Nevertheless, there are syllabi that specify how mathematics is to be taught, and in most such syllabi there is still no place for computer algebra.

Why is that so? Naturally it takes some time for new developments to take their place in the channels of the education system; the curriculum, the school books, the education of teachers. This delay is an important protection mechanism; if every new development were to be implemented post-haste in the school system, then we can only pity the poor student who happens to be in school when some innovation arrives that is later found to be frivolous. A cornerstone of what we call culture is the preservation of standards; only that which has proved itself over an extended period of time, that has been widely appreciated by many people, should be able to make its way into the system.

Without question we live in an information age, accelerating and speeding away. New technologies arrive more and more quickly and the danger of missing opportunities increases. We repeatedly bump up against the limits of adaptability of contemporary social structures and mechanisms. Take, for example, the United Kingdom curriculum and examination system, where the A-levels must be defined more than two years before the examination date. Who can honestly and definitively state which examination aids will be available to a student more than two years from now, or whether the current bans and controls will still make sense or even be enforceable then?

In the past the world of the grandchildren was more or less the same as the world of the grandparents, whereas today there is a difference between the older brother's world and that of the younger sister. Something like "general knowledge" (an essential paradigm of the modern school system) exists only partially today.

The school, as a whole, will have to modify itself in order to do justice to the times in which we find ourselves. The teaching of mathematics will not be immune to these changes. Chapters 3 and 8 are dedicated to looking at what these changes might mean: Chapter 3 gives a picture of how the teaching of mathematics could look in the future, while Chapter 8 compares the (presently closing) industrial age to the birth of the new age of information. Arising from this are interesting, if not confusing, prognoses and prophecies, some of which have already come to pass.

But until then, mathematics will continue to be taught according to existing teaching plans. However there will be more and more schools, teachers and students with access to computer algebra systems, who will (want to) use them. Therefore in this chapter we look at the ways in which computer algebra systems can be incorporated into existing mathematics teaching situations within the boundaries of contemporary syllabi. Teachers who already have one foot in the future will find the changes on their way much easier to deal with.

The House of Mathematics

In order to describe the current state of mathematics teaching, we will use the metaphor of building a house:

- The teacher starts with the teaching of *arithmetic*. This corresponds to building the ground floor.
- Next comes the teaching of *elementary algebra*, corresponding to the first floor. In the same way that the first floor of a building needs a good ground floor to stand upon, the students need a good command of arithmetic before they can start with algebra.
- The next theme, the second storey so to speak, could be the solution of simple linear equations. In order to learn how an equation is solved, one must be able to work in an algebraic setting without difficulties.

And so on. In this way we build up the structure that we refer to as the "House of Mathematics".

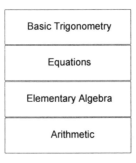

Basic Trigonometry
Equations
Elementary Algebra
Arithmetic

It is obvious that the metaphor of a single building is a rather simple one. In reality, mathematics would be better represented by a collection of buildings, perhaps even a small city. Nevertheless, we remain with the image of a single building, which will be much more useful and is by no means a real limitation.

We now look at two examples that are a common part of teaching and learning. First we look at solving a simple equation, then we look at an applied trigonometry problem.

Example 1: Solving equations

In order to solve the equation

$$5x - 6 = 2x + 15,$$

we require a series of algebraic manipulations that transform the equation into the form

$$x = ...$$

In the search for such a series of manipulations, the following strategy is recommended to students: "first bring all the x's to one side and all the rest to the other side". A good first step is the subtraction of $2x$ from both sides.

$$5x - 6 = 2x + 15 \qquad |-2x$$

From the decision to use this transformation follows the actual application of it to both sides of the equation:

$$5x - 6 - 2x = 2x + 15 - 2x$$
$$3x - 6 = 15$$

Now we select another transformation, the addition of 6 presenting itself.

$$3x - 6 = 15 \qquad\qquad |+6$$

Once again we apply it to both sides of the equation:

$$3x - 6 + 6 = 15 + 6$$
$$3x = 21$$

Analysing the preceding solution method we see two actions alternating:

- The choice of an algebraic transformation.
- The application of this transformation.

The first action, the act of choice, is here of more strategic importance, being the aspect that differentiates the solving of equations from basic algebra. The second action, that of applying the transformation, is of less importance, being essentially a manual operation. The teacher must be able to presuppose that the student can carry this out without problem. (Naturally, at an earlier point in the course, this manual action of applying algebraic transformations had a much more important role.)

If we observe only manual skills, then we see that those required for solving equations can be presented as follows:

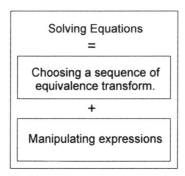

We consciously present only the manual skills in this diagram, ignoring many other skills such as a conceptual understanding of the problem or the recognition of term expressions. This is a concrete (and simplified) example of our "House of Mathematics": a student will only reach the "Solving Equations" storey if the "Expression Rewriting" level is sufficiently well built.

In the process of solving a concrete example there is a constant changing between the strategic and hand labour levels. The primary action of choosing transformations is repeatedly interrupted by the less important manual activity of algebraic manipulation.

This repeated change of focus becomes a source of errors when the activity of algebraic manipulation is not fully mastered. To make this clear, let's go back to the example shown above: we were at the equation $3x = 21$, and we were once again confronted with the problem of choosing an algebraic transformation. Of course *you* know what comes next. But what actually happens in the heads of many beginners? Something like the following thoughts breeze through: "Hmm, 3 in front of the unknown x. So I have to subtract 3 from both sides to get the answer."

$3x = 21 \qquad \qquad |-3$

Then when the student changes down to the manipulation level, the false answer $x = 18$ pops out. Why? Because the subtraction of 3 from both sides is intended to get x= on the left hand side, so the calculation is not actually performed; the student simply writes x=21-3 and is done. Many students simply do not manage the repetitive level change, leading to errors that often are not found, even by later checking.

Example 2: Applied trigonometry problems

Let's imagine a student solving a problem. The problem is:

> On a hill of slope $\varepsilon = 30°$ there is a tree. A 15*m* long straight line
> *AB* is marked out directly downhill from the tree. From *A* the top of
> the tree makes an angle of $\alpha = 40°$ with the hill. From *B* the tree-top
> makes an angle of $\beta = 50°$ with the hill. How high is the tree?

We presume that the student knows about trigonometry in triangles, can use the
sine and cosine laws and thus can fill in the missing quantities in a triangle should
he have enough information presented.

As we know, a picture says more than a thousand words. The first and arguably the
most important step in the solution is the sketching of the problem. (The computer
is still of no direct help in the conversion of a written problem into a diagram.)

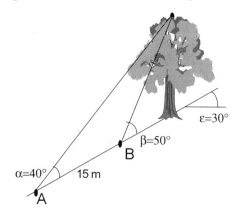

The strategy to solve this problem is to find a sequence of triangles. In each triangle
we calculate the unknown quantities, so that we can then calculate enough
quantities in the next triangle in the sequence. We carry on this process until we
know the quantities we want, in this case the height of the tree. The first triangle
must be one in which we know enough quantities to start. It helps to take the
sketch above, abstract it and give names to all appropriate points and edges.

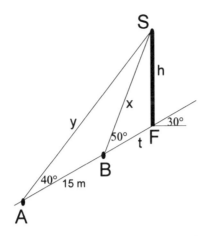

At each point in the solution process the student selects the next triangle to attack, one in which enough information is known. To be successful, the student needs to look out for the following configurations:

- All three side lengths are known.
- Two sides and one (the included) angle are known.
- One side and two angles are known.

None of the three possible triangles *ABS*, *AFS* and *BFS* match one of these cases. In this case we have to use elementary geometric knowledge such as complementary, supplementary or identical angles. Thus the process of solving the problem is rather non-trivial.

Since the angles $\angle ABS$ and $\angle FBS = \beta = 50°$ sum to $180°$, we can calculate the angle $\angle ABS$ as $130°$. Thus in the triangle *ABS* we know one edge length and two angles (the third angle, $\angle ASB$, can be calculated using: $\angle ASB = 180° - 40° - 130° = 10°$). Using the sine law one can now calculate x and y.

$$\frac{x}{\sin(40°)} = \frac{15}{\sin(10°)}, \quad \text{so } x = \frac{15 \cdot \sin(40°)}{\sin(10°)}, \text{ that is, } x = 55.525$$

$$\frac{y}{\sin(130°)} = \frac{15}{\sin(10°)}, \quad \text{so } y = \frac{15 \cdot \sin(130°)}{\sin(10°)}, \text{ that is, } y = 66.172$$

Using the knowledge that $\angle BFS = 90° + \varepsilon = 120°$ we have, in the triangle *BFS*, one edge length (namely x) and two angles (thus all three angles, since $\angle BSF = 180° - 50° - 120° = 10°$). The remaining edge lengths t and h can be similarly calculated:

$$\frac{t}{\sin(10°)} = \frac{x}{\sin(120°)}, \text{ so } t = \frac{x \cdot \sin(10°)}{\sin(120°)}, \text{ that is, } t = 11.133$$

$$\frac{h}{\sin(50°)} = \frac{x}{\sin(120°)}, \text{ so } h = \frac{x \cdot \sin(50°)}{\sin(120°)}, \text{ that is, } h = 49.114$$

Thus we know the height of the tree, a huge 49.1 metres.

This is how a student should go about such a problem. An analysis of the observed solution steps reveals once again two alternating necessary skills:

- The selection of a triangle.
- The calculation of unknown quantities in a triangle.

The first skill, the selection of a triangle, is once again the more important of the two; it is the strategic skill. It is the actual new skill that is taught in an applied trigonometry course. The second skill, calculating unknown quantities in a given triangle (trigonometry), is of less importance.

Again, if we observe only the manual skills, we can reduce the skills necessary to solve applied trigonometry problems as follows:

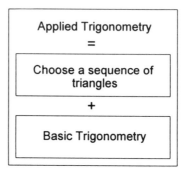

With this example it becomes clearer that the repeated change of levels can condemn to failure those with no great mastery of the lower level. Think once again about the "House of Mathematics" and you will see why so many of your students fail to grasp the idea of applied trigonometry problems. Every student with an insufficiently well built trigonometry storey will be unable to lay even the first row of bricks for further construction. Try the following: a student selects a triangle. Then (s)he must "climb down" and use the just-learnt trigonometry on this triangle, something that takes full concentration. If, not even when, *if* (s)he can carry this out, then (s)he must climb to the upper storey and attempt to regain the much more complex train of thought (s)he lay aside before climbing down. Not all students can easily manage this.

A rather disjointed skill in this process is the use of elementary geometric relations (complementary angles, etc.) to find information about triangles. This skill plays a similar role to the recognition of the syntactic structure of an expression in the solving of equations, directing the student towards selecting appropriate algebraic manipulations.

How do we teach, and how do we learn?

The methodology indicated in the examples above is used predominately in the teaching of mathematics as follows. In a first phase a skill A is taught and trained (in the examples above, trigonometry or basic algebraic manipulation). Then, in a second phase, a skill B is taught and trained (e.g. choice of transformation or selection of appropriate triangles), that is a main part of a third skill (e.g. solution of equations or applied trigonometry problems). Usually B builds upon A such that in the learning of B one exercises the previously learnt skill A.

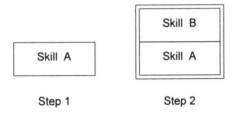

In this method, a student can give only so much attention and concentration to the learning of the skill B, as (s)he has competence in the skill A. Thus this method is inappropriate for those students who have not yet achieved a mastery of skill A when the teaching of skill B starts (often the majority of students in a class!). To remain with our metaphor, it is as though we wanted to build a new storey above an unfinished, fragmentary one.

The "House of Mathematics" that we introduced at the beginning of this chapter is the ideal, utopian vision of the teacher: *beautiful, clean and complete*. From the point of view of the student, there is a somewhat different picture: in the process of learning mathematics over a number of years, each one builds a personal "House of Mathematics", assembled one storey at a time under the supervision of various teachers. When the teacher stops working on some subject, the storey is often nowhere near finished for the student. Each has various gaps and holes in the walls and other structures of this storey, and each student has them in different places.

At this point it would be ideal for every student to receive some special tutoring to fill the gaps and to plug the holes in their learning. For such utopianism there is, unfortunately, no time; the teacher must move on to the next subject in the syllabus. As to how the teachers go on, the question remains as to how to proceed without losing the students, especially those with exceptionally large and structurally important gaps.

Building a house with DERIVE

If we want to build on a house that is not yet finished, to add a second storey before the first is completed, we use a scaffold to support the new structure until the first storey is ready to hold the weight.

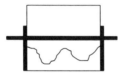

This idea can be pressed into our service as follows: first we teach the skill A and exercise it somewhat. When we start with a new skill, we delegate the solution of sub-problems that require skill A (such as algebraic manipulation or the calculation of unknown quantities in a triangle) to a computer, which thus acts as scaffolding between the A and B storeys.

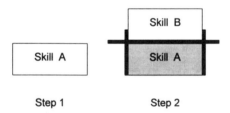

This idea originates with Prof. Bruno Buchberger, head of the Austrian Research Institute for Symbolic Computation (RISC-Linz/Hagenberg), who called it the *White-Box/Black-Box Principle*. To start, skill A is a White Box, and is taught and exercised without any computer assistance. When skill B becomes the focus of teaching, and thus skill A appears only as a method to solve certain sub-problems, skill A becomes a Black Box. That is, skill A is used with help of a computer. As an illustration of this concept we will look at the above examples using this method.

First we solve the equation $5x - 6 = 2x + 15$, where the user is responsible for the choice of algebraic manipulations and DERIVE takes over the effort required for applying these manipulations. We start with the input of the equation.

❑ [A]uthor 5x-6=2x+15 [↵]

```
#1:   5·x – 6 = 2·x + 15
```

With the [F4] key we copy the expression in parentheses into the input. In order to apply the manipulation $-2x$, one must input

❑ [A]uthor [F4]-2x [↵]

```
#2:   (5·x – 6 = 2·x + 15) – 2·x
```

Thus the choice of manipulation is given to the user (i.e. the student). The application of that manipulation is then delegated to DERIVE.

❑ [S]implify [↵]

```
#3:   3·x – 6 = 15
```

The student then inputs the next manipulation

❑ [A]uthor [F4]+6 [↵]

```
#4:   (3·x – 6 = 15) + 6
```

and again delegates the application to the computer.

❑ [S]implify [↵]

```
#5:   3·x = 21
```

So far, so good. A student who would have then proceeded with the above mentioned false step would proceed as follows:

❑ [A]uthor [F4]-3 [↵]

   [S]implify [↵]

```
#6:   (3·x = 21) – 3

#7:   3·x – 3 = 18
```

That the result is not the expected $x=$ (and given that he trusts in the accuracy of the computation!), indicates to the student that the selected manipulation was not the correct one, and another must be attempted.

This method has two fundamental advantages:

- The student concentrates on the principal skill being learnt, the selection of appropriate algebraic manipulations.
- The student receives *immediate* feedback as to the appropriateness of the selected manipulation in light of the strategy. Thus trial and error learning takes place as a side-effect. In many experiments with Austrian schoolchildren this was found to be very effective.

In the solution of the applied trigonometry problems similar effects occur. First let's look at the sketch again:

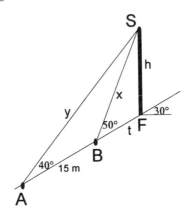

In this example the student takes on the responsibility of selecting appropriate triangles, while the computer takes care of the trigonometry. The function TRIANGLE takes as arguments the three sides and the three (respectively opposite) angles and returns, where possible, the unknown quantities. This function is not one of DERIVE's standards, but was programmed by the author and "knows" the rules of trigonometry in triangles.

The student starts by selecting the triangle *ABS* and enters the known quantities as arguments to the TRIANGLE function.

❑ [A]uthor `triangle(15,x,y,10°,40°,130°)` [↵]

```
#1:  TRIANGLE(15, x, y, 10·°, 40·°, 130·°)
```

Of course only two angles are actually necessary, but it is not necessary to give only the minimal information at all times. The application of the ›Simplify‹ command forces the calculation of the triangle quantities.

❑ [S]implify [↵]

```
#2:  [x = 55.525, y = 66.172]
```

The student then chooses the triangle *BFS* and uses again the TRIANGLE function and the ›Simplify‹ command.

❑   Ⓐuthor `triangle(55.525,t,h,120°,10°,50°)` ⏎

   Ⓢimplify ⏎

```
#3:   TRIANGLE(55.525, t, h, 120·°, 10·°, 50·°)

#4:   [t = 11.133, h = 49.114]
```

Thanks to the function TRIANGLE the student can concentrate almost exclusively on the skill to be learnt, namely the selection of triangles.

The method of delegating tasks to a computer is already well established in one part of modern school mathematics, the use of calculators as scaffolding over the arithmetic storey. First students learn to calculate by hand. At some point (ideally selected by the teacher) the students learn to use a calculator. On one hand, it saves time and thus allows more complex and interesting examples to be dealt with. On the other hand, it allows those students who constantly make arithmetic mistakes, or who otherwise have gaps in their arithmetic storey, to proceed onto the next level of mathematics. Thus through the existence of the scaffolding element known as a calculator, it is no longer necessary to be a wizard in calculating by hand before one can go on to deal with further subjects in mathematics.

Computer algebra systems allow the extension of this scaffolding method to most areas of school mathematics. Independent studies in the UK, Germany and Austria have shown that up to 80% of what is required for school-leaving, respectively A-levels, Bacalaureat, Abitur and Matura, can be automated with DERIVE

Thus all students, regardless of how complete or fragmentary their personal "House of Mathematics" is, can participate in more advanced and interesting areas of mathematics. Especially those students who repeatedly miscalculate although they have a good understanding of the material, thus achieving only mediocre results, can count on DERIVE as a valuable, reassuring "builder's labourer".

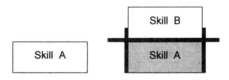

The use of a computer is not always the appropriate solution to a lack of skill. Each storey must be sufficiently well built before the assembly of scaffolding can be rationally defended. One example of a minimal level of construction is the conceptual understanding of an operation: a student should not be reaching for the square root key on a calculator before the operation is understood, to the level of knowing when and how it should be used. Here we see the emergence of a new field of education research: What line should we follow for "Construction with computer algebra scaffolding"? At what point should or could an operation become automated, i.e., be converted to a Black Box? The age-old bugbear of determining whether a student has a proper conceptual understanding of a subject rears its (ugly) head once again.

These restrictions are a fundamental part of the intelligent use of computer algebra systems in schools. They are a part of the reason teachers, instead of being made superfluous by computer algebra systems, become more central in the teaching of mathematics. On one hand there is the important and highly non-trivial task of teaching and assisting in the correct use of these tools. On the other hand, there is much more focus and attention to be applied to the aspects of mathematics that cannot be automated. More on this aspect in Chapter 3.

To learn and practise skills A and B independently from one another is comparable to a successful method in body building: the athlete does bicep and tricep exercises consecutively instead of simultaneously. A good athlete then trains both muscles together so as to harmonise their workings. Such work and training phases should also exist in mathematics. More of this in the next section.

Scaffolding

If we were to comprehensively implement the White-Box/Black-Box Principle as mentioned above, there would exist the not insignificant danger that many students would be unable to do any mathematics without the help of a computer. In other words, it is possible that a student's "House of Mathematics" would consist entirely of scaffolding, that the student relies completely upon the existence of scaffolding, that is, upon the efficiency of the computer. That cannot and must not be the goal of mathematics teaching; it would be completely irresponsible. The methods described above are thus to be modified and changed to suit local conditions.

For those skills that are fundamental for a student, for instance those that are to be directly tested at the examinations at the end of high school, a consolidation phase after the above mentioned phases 1 and 2 is necessary, where the student must then practise solving problems without any assistance from a computer. Thus we add a third phase where we solve problems in the same way that we do now, i.e., by hand. This is similar to the bodybuilder who adds special exercises to his routine to use whole groups of muscles together.

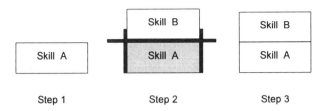

Step 1   Step 2   Step 3

For even more important skills, the student could build the scaffold at the end of Phase 1 herself. For instance the TRIANGLE function from above could be written by the student in DERIVE. It is generally felt that one learns more by programming every detail of a skill than is possible by any other method.

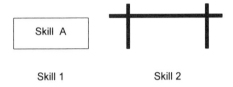

Skill 1   Skill 2

In any case, the other end of the scale is easy to see: many skills are easily removed from the syllabus, it being sufficient that one can use a calculator to obtain the right answer. A simple example of this is the square root. The algorithm to calculate it is rarely taught; students and teachers alike resort immediately to the calculator. In such cases, the computer can be immediately pressed into service as scaffolding.

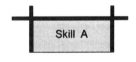

Skill 1

Another method arises; from the start we teach skill A with the scaffold in place, building the storey from the top and bottom simultaneously. This can be done in many ways through alternating computer usage with non-computer methods. Successful teaching experiments were undertaken in England, where the introduction of differential calculus was accompanied by experiments using the still unknown DERIVE command ›Calculus Differentiate‹. The students have discovered the first differential rules themselves and were thus motivated to start with the classical approach to the theme. This method could also be called the Black-Box/White-Box Principle.

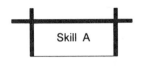

Step 1

One observes in many cases that a fragmentary storey becomes complete over time due to the security that the scaffolding affords. One could see this as a form of self-completion or self-repair.

In all, we have six methods of teaching. Method 1 is the traditional method, Methods 2-6 will be collectively referred to as "Scaffolding".

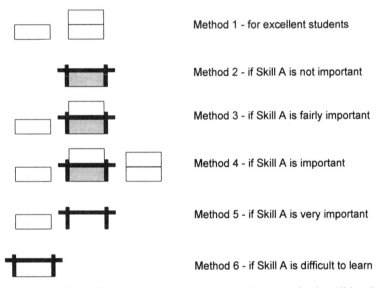

Method 1 - for excellent students

Method 2 - if Skill A is not important

Method 3 - if Skill A is fairly important

Method 4 - if Skill A is important

Method 5 - if Skill A is very important

Method 6 - if Skill A is difficult to learn

The importance of a skill, and thus the optimal teaching method, will be dependent upon the teaching plan and the type of school. Trigonometry could be taught by Method 3 for trade schools and by Methods 4 or 5 for students heading towards university or other further education. For some skills it will still depend upon the actual class that the teacher is dealing with.

The advantage of tools such as DERIVE lies in the options that become available to a teacher, and that the teacher can then choose in which way the tool is presented. Computer algebra systems open new chances and possibilities for teaching (namely Methods 2-6 above) and the teacher can then decide which is most appropriate.

A different view: DERIVE as mathematical spectacles

Tools can serve us as amplifiers of our natural capabilities, as a telescope allows us to see further than with the naked eye. Or they can compensate for temporary or permanent disabilities, as spectacles correct long- or short-sightedness. DERIVE can take on both aspects: for gifted students (or practising mathematicians), DERIVE acts as an amplifier, accelerating calculations and improving their accuracy. For more average students DERIVE is a way of reaching the capabilities that the more gifted students have naturally.

As a pair of glasses can compensate for physical weaknesses, so can DERIVE, in collaboration with the right methods, compensate for mathematical weaknesses. To prevent students with an obvious weakness in calculation from using a tool such as DERIVE is comparable to forbidding short-sighted people to wear glasses. In the same way that almost every person (except the blind) can see clearly, some naturally, others with glasses, almost everyone (except an unfortunate few), given the right tools and the right instruction, can reach a good level of mathematical understanding and competence.

Before we spring into the future of mathematics teaching, we close with two more aspects that argue for the use of computer algebra systems in a contemporary curriculum:

- It is a standard method in mathematics that once something is worked out, it is applied afterwards without repeating all the work. Once a theorem is proved, the results are used in later theorems without proving the result once again. Using this Module, Macro or Black-Box Principle would introduce the students to a useful method of mathematics.
- The use of computer tools requires absolute syntactic accuracy; every forgotten parenthesis is signalled as an error. The computer is more unsympathetic than any teacher could hope to be. On one hand the use of a computer reinforces the need for mathematical exactness, something that must remain a goal of mathematics; on the other hand, the teacher must not act as the pedantic "dot your i's and cross your t's" discipliner, rather the teacher becomes a partner in the battle with the merciless machine.

CHAPTER 3

THE FUTURE OF MATHEMATICS TEACHING

Tools such as DERIVE make fundamental changes, slicing clean through the landscape of current teaching principles. There will be no single future for all students, teachers and schools; geographical and cultural variation as well as differing aims of schools will increase the plurality. Thus we cannot aim for a comprehensive vision of the future, rather we present food for thought, a veritable banquet of possibilities for new approaches to mathematics. We prepare the ground with a discussion of the question:

What is Mathematics?

Many important researchers have discussed this question. First to Bertrand Russell, who characterised mathematics thus:

> "Mathematics may be defined as the subject in which we never know what we are talking about, nor whether what we are saying is true."

That sounds somewhat surprising. Should mathematics be in some sense divorced from reality? Many people claim and believe almost religiously that mathematics is the tool of truth. So let's get a second opinion. David Hilbert, the man who finally placed geometry on a solid basis two thousand years after Euclid, thus helping found modern axiomatic mathematics (and also modern logic), said:

> "One must be able to say at all times - instead of points, lines and planes - tables, chairs and beermugs."

Here we have something similar to Russell's comment. Both these opinions refer to something that we now know as as *pure mathematics*; mathematics for its own sake, mathematics as cerebral fitness.

This is but one side of mathematics. The other, pragmatic, aspect of mathematics deals with the solving of real-world problems. To solve some problem P, one proceeds as follows:

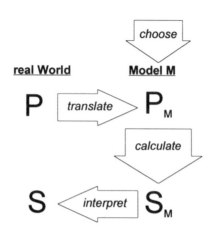

- Step 1: Select a suitable model M.
- Step 2: Translate the real-world problem P into a model problem P_M.
- Step 3: From the model problem P_M, calculate a model solution S_M.
- Step 4: Interpret the model solution S_M to obtain a real-world solution S.

A simple example would help. Let the problem P be: "two children, born two years apart, have ages that sum to 8 years. How old is each child?". As a model we use equations in two variables. The translation of the problem, P_M, is $\{x + y = 8, x - y = 2\}$. A calculation, specifically the solution of these two equations, gives the model solution $S_M = \{x = 5, y = 3\}$. The interpretation gives the real-world solution: "the children are 3 and 5 years old".

Often we have to iterate these steps. If, for instance, the interpreted actual solution L is not appropriate as a solution (e.g. it is too inaccurate or unfeasible), then there are various possible causes for this. Perhaps we took the wrong model, or we forgot some important detail in the translation, or perhaps we simply performed an incorrect calculation. In all cases we must start again from the beginning.

This sort of mathematics, the interface between the real world and a more abstract world, is known as *applied mathematics*.

What sort of mathematics should we be teaching in the future? A new form of instruction, using new tools that change both teaching and learning, would embrace the following:

- Mathematics as a problem solving art: the solution of problems is one of the foundations of human nature, one of the skills that are used in almost every situation.

- Mathematics as a cerebral workout: in an era where computers take on much of our mental workload, we must ensure that our intellectual powers do not atrophy.
- Mathematics as culture: mathematical and cultural developments have always occurred hand in hand. Mathematics is an integral part of our civilisation; an understanding of mathematics helps us understand our culture.

With these goals in mind, we present over the next few sections many proposals for new ways of presenting mathematics, both in form and content. But first a short aside.

Let's take the quotation from Bertrand Russell, "Mathematics may be defined as the subject in which we never know what we are talking about, nor whether what we are saying is true," and look at it once again with reference to the diagram:

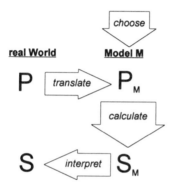

Russell makes a clear distinction between the mathematical model and the real world. The mathematical formulation and solution of real problems are as good (in the sense of being usable) or bad (unusable) as the chosen translation of the problem. There are cast iron proofs of truth or falsity inside mathematical models, but none for the validity of a translation. The accuracy, relevance or usefulness of a given interpretation will always remain a question of point of view, and will remain controversial even among experts.

"Mathematical calculations have shown..." is one of the most awe-inspiring phrases of our time but, considering the preceding discussion, without reason. This phrase is used in order to sell something as an indubitable and unchangeable fact. The truth is that the whole accuracy or lack thereof lies in the interpretation of the mathematical calculations. Statistics are the classic example.

It should be a goal of mathematics teaching to make the limits of mathematical reasoning clear, to free the subject from the mystical aura that threatens to suffocate.

Cleaning out

What can we omit? Let's first look at the current state of the nation. The four major skills for problem solving receive the following amounts of time in current teaching:

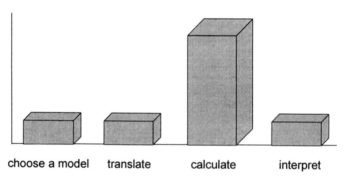

The most time is given over to calculations and the teaching of calculating skills. Modern mathematics teaching is thus mainly an education for intellectual hand-workers. There are two causes for concern arising from this state of affairs:

- Firstly, most calculating skills can be more efficiently and accurately carried out by computer systems (for instance DERIVE).
- Secondly, most students will never need these particular skills again in their lives. The often heard complaint "Where will I ever need this?" is justified.

Is there a value in solving a problem such as $\dfrac{d}{dx}\left(\sqrt{e^{x^2}+\sin(3x^2+4)}\cdot\cos(\ln(7x^3))\right)$?

Except as a brain workout it has no purpose. Even as a fitness test it seems pretty pointless. Instead of demanding three backward somersaults with a twist it would make more sense to stay with simple exercises, say sit-ups and push-ups, done properly.

The clear out should thus start with calculation skills. "Less time for calculation and more for modelling, translation and interpretation", would be our basic recommendation, so that all the aspects of problem solving receive equal attention:

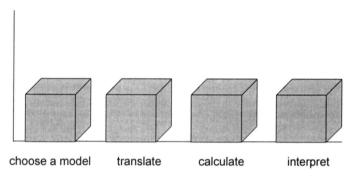

| choose a model | translate | calculate | interpret |

Even with less exercising of the manual skills of calculation, the level of problems that can be solved will not diminish, as there will be computer algebra systems at hand to help. In fact, the same, if not even more difficult and interesting problems can be dealt with.

Taking into account the possibilities of the Scaffolding, we need to pay careful attention to each individual calculating skill and to examine its relevance, modifying the amount of time spent in teaching accordingly. In the process of clearing out, the following two aspects are of prime importance (dependent upon local needs, of course):

- In most subject areas, the teaching of a skill has many side-effects, often ones that have more to do with conceptual understanding. If a student, for instance, solves an equation using step-by-step transformations, then (s)he learns about the structure of a term as a side-effect. In the case that a side-effect is important and is not dealt with by other means, then the skill cannot be done away with. Often one must resort to Method 3 of the Scaffolding:

- Calculating skills are a safety net for some students, often being a guarantee of passing an examination. In an examination situation, many students immediately go to those (sub-)problems that involve only the (mechanical) skills of differentiating, transforming or simplifying an expression. What should happen to these students? Some will achieve a better understanding of mathematics because the teacher will have more time to concentrate on the teaching and training of concepts necessary for problem solving. For others new safety nets must be constructed. Perhaps the history of mathematics could be such a subject.

We will now look more closely at two concrete subjects. Since an analysis depends on so many local factors (from teaching traditions via the curriculum to school-specific necessities), we must leave the actual fitting to each teacher.

Curve discussions: The reason that we perform curve discussions is to obtain information about the important points on a curve. If one wants to plot a decent graph, then one must ensure that the intercepts, extreme values and points of inflection are accurately represented. Curve discussions were thus always preparation for the plotting of a graph. Graphic calculators or the ›Plot‹ command in DERIVE make this preparation unnecessary, in that they make the plotting of graphs trivial. But there is an important side-effect of curve discussions, namely the experiencing of the connections between the graph and the curve, e.g. between the extreme values and the zeroes of the first derivative. Thus curve discussions should not disappear completely. In the future curve discussions might be taught with this side effect as the main goal. Up to now, this side effect was often not emphasised due to the concentration on the calculations.

Decomposition of a fraction into partial fractions: Decomposing fractions has been taught until now in preparation for the study of integration. DERIVE can integrate practically every example that is found in contemporary teaching, in the process it decomposes fractions itself. The decomposition can also be performed explicitly using the ›Expand‹ command. The following example of a rational function required a half second computation time on a 33MHz-PC-486:

$$\#1: \quad \frac{4 \cdot x^8 - 3 \cdot x^7 + 25 \cdot x^6 - 11 \cdot x^5 + 18 \cdot x^4 - 9 \cdot x^3 + 8 \cdot x^2 - 3 \cdot x + 1}{3 \cdot x^9 - 2 \cdot x^8 + 7 \cdot x^7 - 4 \cdot x^6 + 5 \cdot x^5 - 2 \cdot x^4 + x^3}$$

$$\#2: \quad \frac{4 \cdot x}{3 \cdot x^2 - 2 \cdot x + 1} + \frac{3 \cdot x}{(x^2 + 1)^2} + \frac{2}{(x^2 + 1)^2} - \frac{x}{x^2 + 1} + \frac{1}{x^3} - \frac{1}{x^2} + \frac{1}{x}$$

There is no real need to teach this skill in the future. The question of whether the decomposition of fractions has some other side-effect has not, as far as we know, been given a decent positive answer. We thus recommend that this skill be removed from future syllabuses, being reduced to a position similar to the square root, where the calculation skill is not taught at all. Where necessary a computer can be used to obtain the required answer.

After cleaning out we have free space. This space should be used intelligently. We subdivide the process of reformulating mathematics teaching into the following areas:

- Concentration upon the critical points of education.
- Adding new syllabus subjects.
- Adding new teaching methods.
- Adding new educational goals.

These four points are discussed in separate sections below. Some of the ideas contained therein might appear rather revolutionary to some readers. This is intentional: we want to sketch a full and general picture, in the knowledge that changes can only occur in tiny steps. Certainly, before one sets off on a journey, one should know where one is heading. We furnish a vision of the goal of our journey in this chapter.

Many of the following educational ideas require not only no computer algebra systems, but not even a computer. The changes brought about by these new technologies will lead to a style of mathematics teaching that has much less reliance on computers. The reason for this is that there is no automation possible for many mathematical skills. Even when it sounds paradoxical, it is so: the educational innovation bought about by a computer is the redundancy of the computer. DERIVE automates up to 80% of what is currently taught as mathematics. But the resulting minimisation of that part of the syllabus leads to a new formulation so that DERIVE can only help with, at most, 20% of it.

This message will reassure every teacher who shuns the use of computers in teaching because they fear that the students will easily surpass their ability to use the machine: we teachers will increasingly concentrate on the skills that differentiate us from computers!

We must keep the ambitions of education politicians in mind. The news that a computer can automate 80% of contemporary school mathematics could easily lead to the politically motivated idea that a computer supported mathematics education should be possible within only one half the presently allotted time. In an age when talk of budget trimming and cutbacks is rampant, this is no idle fear. Thus we need to modify mathematics teaching in ways which we see fit, so that it maintains a decent existence, before the modifications are performed by others.

Concentration upon the critical points of education

In the incremental education that leads to a general mathematical understanding there are certain elements upon which subsequent themes depend significantly. In the metaphor of the "House of Mathematics", these are the particularly important storeys.

These themes should occupy disproportionately large amounts of space in a future curriculum. In the following we enumerate five such, in our view, important themes. As an example we concentrate on two of these.

Rational and irrational numbers

Calculating with rational and irrational numbers is an important preparation as much for the calculation of algebraic expressions as for the use of various representations of objects. Manipulating fractions, cancelling common factors, bringing them over a common denominator, multiplying numerator and denominator by a factor, turning a fraction of fractions into a fraction of integers - these use the same skills that one needs to manipulate terms containing variables. The conversion between fractions and decimal numbers as well as the determination as to which representation is more appropriate and what limits exist with the chosen representation, all this has a lot to do with the use of various representations of objects.

The calculator has had the unfortunate effect that students replace all numbers, rational and irrational, with decimal approximations and perform all calculations with the calculator. From this two disadvantages arise:

- One relinquishes exact results and introduces unnecessary rounding errors. These rounding errors can grow to significant proportions.
- One deprives oneself of the possibility of practising those skills that are necessary for the transformation of algebraic expressions.

The teacher needs to fight against this trend and insist, as far as possible, on exact results. As well as the traditional methods, we can use DERIVE for this. The following exercises work towards an understanding of term structure. First the student enters an expression given by the teacher, e.g., $1 - \dfrac{2}{\sqrt{3}+4}$:

❏ [A]uthor 1-2/(√3+4) = [↵]

```
        2
#1:  1 - ─────
        √3 + 4
```

The input occurs in one dimension, so that certain parts (here the denominator) must be entered in brackets. Since DERIVE prints the expression two-dimensionally, the student can easily check whether that which he entered is the same as that which the teacher intended.

Then the student is asked to create - using the same sequence of numbers and operations, but other bracketing - as many different values as possible, e.g.:

❏ [A]uthor 1-2/√3+4= [↵]

   [A]uthor 1-(2/(√3+4))= [↵]

   [A]uthor (1-2)/√3+4= [↵]

   [A]uthor (1-2)/(√3+4)= [↵]

Some of these attempts will lead to the same number, which is an opportunity to discuss why some brackets are unnecessary.

Next the student is called upon to use the arrow keys to home in on a given subexpression, attempting to reach it in the least number of steps, e.g.:

❏ [←] [↓] [→]

```
        2
#3:  1 - ─────
        √3 + 4
```

A further useful exercise is the stepwise evaluation of an expression. For example, let the following expression be given (either the student enters the expression herself or it is loaded using the ›Transfer Load Derive‹ command from a teacher-prepared file):

```
        2 - 1
#1:  1 + ─────
        2 + 1
```

The student then receives the following instructions:

(1) Home in on a subexpression that contains the least possible number of operations and has not already been tried.

(2) Invoke the ›Simplify‹ command.

(3) Repeat steps (1) and (2), until no further changes can be made.

In the process it is to be noted how many steps are necessary. Only those steps where something has changed count. Who can manage the least number of steps? For the example above it could proceed as follows:

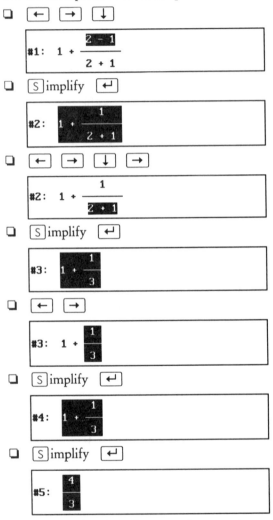

After a couple of similar examples questions could be posed along the following lines: "are there cases where simplification makes no change to an expression? If so, can you determine these cases before applying the ›Simplify‹ command?".

The ›approX‹ command is a useful tool for the comparison of fractions and decimal numbers. With it we can discuss the benefits and limitations of the two representations. For instance comparing decimals is easier than comparing fractions.

❑ [A]uthor 14/23<19/31 [↵]

   appro[X] [↵]

```
        14       19
#1:    ---  <   ---
        23       31

#2:   0.608695 < 0.612903
```

But it is not necessary to convert to decimals. Instead one can multiply expression #1 by both denominators and simplify the result. This gives exact results.

❑ [A]uthor #1*23*31 [↵]

   [S]implify [↵]

```
        ┌  14       19  ┐
#3:     | ---  <   --- |·23·31
        └  23       31  ┘

#4:   434 < 437
```

It is very informative to show the limits of usefulness of decimals: which number is larger, $\dfrac{20576}{164609}$ or $\dfrac{1}{8}$?

❑ [A]uhor 20576/164609 < 1/8 [↵]

   appro[X] [↵]

```
        20576       1
#5:    ------  <   ---
       164609       8

#6:   0.125 < 0.125
```

The conversion to decimals leads to the same result in both cases. Are the two values actually identical? We try the exact method as an alternative, multiplying by the two denominators:

❑ [A]uthor #5*164609*8 [↵]

   [S]implify [↵]

```
        ┌  20576       1  ┐
#7:     | ------  <   --- |·164609·8
        └  164609       8  ┘

#8:   164608 < 164609
```

The two values are thus not equal! Why did the ›approX‹ command return the same value in both cases? Well, of all possible numbers there are only a few that can be represented with a finite number of decimal places. Since we only have a finite number of digits to work with when we enter or compute with decimal numbers, there will almost always be tiny errors that can lead to such problems as shown above. In comparison to a calculator, however, one can tell DERIVE how many decimal places to use in calculations (6 digits is the default). We convert expression #5 again, but with 15 significant digits this time. The APPROX function meets this need:

❑   [A]uthor   approx(#5,15)   [↵]

    [S]implify   [↵]

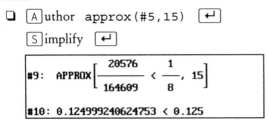

```
                 ⎡ 20576       1      ⎤
#9:  APPROX ⎢ ─────── < ─── , 15⎥
                 ⎣ 164609      8      ⎦

#10: 0.124999240624753 < 0.125
```

With fifteen significant digits the decimals are different and one can tell which is the smaller value. What happens however when the difference appears first at the three-thousandth digit? This characteristic danger with decimals is the price we pay for their (often extremely comfortable) use. By experimenting with the computer, students can come to understand and look into this important fact themselves.

Variables

What is a variable? What does an expression like $x^2 - 1$ actually mean? Is it a virtual object that manifests itself when x is replaced by a concrete value? Or is it the collection of all possible manifestations, when one imagines all possible values replacing x? (This corresponds to that which will later come to be known as a function.)

Much time needs to be allocated for the introduction of such an important concept. DERIVE can help at the beginning, in that it allows the students to discover some of the rules themselves.

❑   [A]uthor   x+x=   [↵]

    [A]uthor   2x+3x=   [↵]

```
#1:  x + x = 2·x

#2:  2·x + 3·x = 5·x
```

❑ [A]uthor x*x= [↵]

[A]uthor 2x*3x= [↵]

```
           2
#3:  x·x = x

              2
#4:  2·x·3·x = 6·x
```

Further exercises in structure recognition could be made, similar to those in the previous section. In certain cases one would replace variables with one or more different values.

With such experiments there are no limits to the imagination. The major beneficial effect is that the rules one discovers for oneself remain in memory much better than those learnt parrot-fashion.

Representations

Representations play a central role in mathematics. Various representations are like various points of view. A city appears completely different when viewed from above, perhaps from the basket of a hot-air balloon, to how it does when viewed from a neighbouring mountain, and different again when viewed by someone taking a walk around the city itself.

If a question about an object is posed, one should take a point of view that makes it as simple as possible to find the answer. To find the quickest way from the council house to the city gasworks one uses the hot-air balloon point of view (that we obtain in the form of a city map). The question as to the tallest building in the city is easily answered from the neighbouring mountain, while the colour of the main door of the church is most easily answered from within the city itself.

One of the basic techniques of mathematics is to find a representation (i.e. a model) of a problem that makes the problem easy to solve, if not actually making the solution obvious. We have already seen this technique above with the comparison of two fractions. A further, easily followed example is as follows:

A cube hangs by a thread attached to one corner. It is otherwise free to move. When we look at this configuration from the front (as in the following picture), then we see the cube as three parallelograms. What is the smallest angle through which we must spin the cube so that we see the same figure?

Trivially we get the same figure after rotating the cube a full 360°, but does it happen earlier? We vary the representation of this problem in that we use a new point of view: we look from above, where the thread attaches. Then we see the following figure:

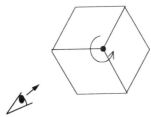

From this point of view the cube always looks the same after an arbitrary rotation, only the position relative to the diagrammed eye changes. Now the answer to the posed question is obvious: for a rotation of 120°, 240° or 360° the figure remains the same for the eye.

A Chinese proverb:

> "If you have a problem, there are two paths open to you: either you solve the problem, or you change your view."

Through changing the view in the above example, the problem character of the situation was lost and the solution became obvious. With such examples the essential understanding of the pros and cons of various representations of a single object can be made clear to students.

Good examples for the subject of representations are the so-called *Drudels*. A Drudel is a picture where one hardly recognises what is pictured, because a "bad" representation of the object has been chosen. Here is an example: what does one see in the following picture?

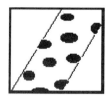

Answer: A giraffe walking in front of an open window.

In mathematics we use three principal types of representation: algebraic, numeric and graphic. DERIVE, with all its possibilities, is a particularly useful tool when it comes to comparison and simultaneous usage of these representations. In the following screen dump we see an object in six representations:

- Expression #1 is the algebraic representation of an expanded polynomial.
- Expression #2 is the algebraic representation in rational factorised form.
- Expression #3 is the algebraic representation in radical factorised form.
- Expression #5 is a table representation for $-1.5 \le x \le 1.5$.
- In window #2 is a graphic representation with same-scale axes.
- In window #3 is a graphic representation with differently scaled axes.

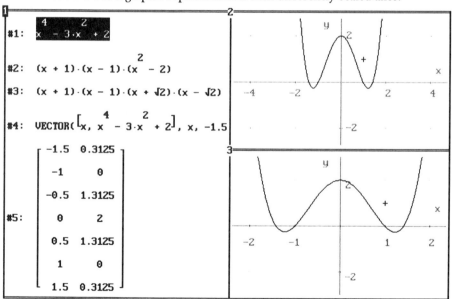

In a juxtaposition of term and graph, as in the above picture, it becomes clear that information about particular points (zeros, axis intersections, extreme values, saddle points) is easier to comprehend with the graphic at hand. Those things that one sees immediately in a graphic representation used to have to be found via a curve discussion, in which several derivatives have to be taken and various equations have to be solved, i.e., a significant amount of work had to be performed.

It is particularly comfortable and useful when one can, as in DERIVE, interact directly with the graphical representation. The graphic representation of an object allows a certain vividness and, in the eyes of the student, a certain usefulness, when one can zoom into particular points on the curve with the graphics cross, reading off certain values or using arbitrary plot frames.

With directions as follows a student can be animated to use the interactive possibilities:

(1) Plot the graph of $x^3 + 3/2\,x^2 - 3/2\,x - 1$.
(2) Describe verbally the special points that you recognise.
(3) Switch (with $\boxed{\text{F3}}$) into trace mode, move to the special points with the graphics box and note the coordinates. Use the ›Range‹ command to enlarge the region around the special points. This increases the accuracy of the reading of coordinates. The goal is three decimal places.
(4) Zoom out several times (with $\boxed{\text{F10}}$) in order to be sure that all special points have been found.

In the context of representations one compares algebraic, numeric and graphic methods for the solution of a problem, e.g. to determine the zeroes of a polynomial.

Functions

The idea of a function is also central to mathematics and deserves a thorough treatment that extends far beyond what is presented in this subject today.

The DERIVE programming language is strongly functional and offers itself as an excellent experimental tool for this subject. The definition of a function, the calculation of function values and the plotting of function graphs are as simple as possible.

❑ $\boxed{\text{A}}$uthor $\texttt{f(x):=(x^2-4)/((x+1)^2(x-2))}$ $\boxed{\hookleftarrow}$

$$\text{\#1:}\quad F(x) := \frac{x^2 - 4}{(x+1)^2 \cdot (x-2)}$$

$\boxed{\text{A}}$uthor $\texttt{f(1)=}$ $\boxed{\hookleftarrow}$

$\boxed{\text{A}}$uthor $\texttt{f(2)=}$ $\boxed{\hookleftarrow}$

#2: $F(1) = \dfrac{3}{4}$

#3: $F(2) = ?$

⬆ ⬆ (to highlight expression #1)

[P]lot [B]eside [↵]

[P]lot

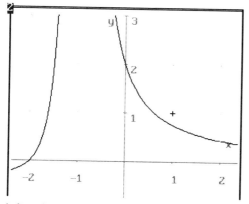

To define functions there are: an IF- function, an iteration function, many selector functions and the technique of recursion. One can also work with general non-specific functions, as in the following example:

❑ [A]uthor g(x) := [↵]

[A]uthor h(x) := [↵]

[A]uthor dif(g(x)*h(x),x) = [↵]

#4: G(x) :=

#5: H(x) :=

#6: $\dfrac{d}{dx}(G(x) \cdot H(x)) = H(x) \cdot \dfrac{d}{dx} G(x) + G(x) \cdot \dfrac{d}{dx} H(x)$

If the concept of various representations of an object has been sufficiently developed, then the idea of functions can also be introduced using the possibilities available via the graphics window. We will develop these themes in detail in a further book.

Limits

The concept of limit values and convergence are of central importance in mathematics, on them we build the whole of analysis using the infinitesimal method. The two concepts play a central role in the understanding of infinities and are, so to speak, the tickets to the world of higher mathematics.

Parallel to the established introduction to this theme one can find new ways that are only possible with a tool such as DERIVE. For example the classic story of *Achilles and the Tortoise* is an excellent introduction to the subject of limits. We propose the following methodology, where we replace Achilles with the US sprinter Carl Lewis and the Tortoise with an average citizen who goes by the name of Alois Black.

> "Carl Lewis and Alois Black compete against one another in a 100 metre dash. Carl runs 100 metres in 10 seconds, Alois needs 20. Carl gives Alois a head-start of 10 metres. How many seconds after the start, and at what position, will Carl pass Alois? "

Then the students receive a demonstration of a solution to this problem using the computer:

From the general time-distance formula $s(t) = v \cdot t + t_0$ we can determine specific time-distance formulae for Carl and Alois. From the text above we can see that Carl has a speed of 10 m/sec, while Alois manages 5 m/sec. For Carl $t_0 = 0$, since he starts by the 0 metre mark. For Alois, with his 10 metre headstart, $t_0 = 10$. The time-distance formulae are then:

❑ Ⓐuthor `d_carl(t):=10t` ⏎

  Ⓐuthor `d_alois(t):=10+5t` ⏎

The graphs are plotted (left picture).

Using Ⓢcale the scaling is altered to `'x:2 y:10'` (right picture).

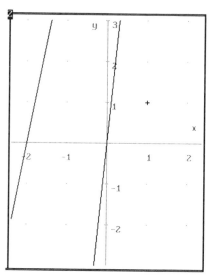 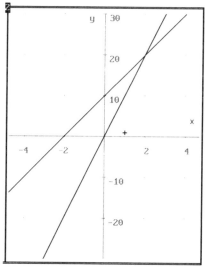

The intersection of the two graphs signifies that Carl overtakes Alois (here we see an ideal point to make a small digression to discuss the relationship between the real problem, the algebraic definition of the problem and the graphic representation of the problem). The coordinates of the intersection give the time and place of overtaking. With the graphics cross the two values can be easily found.

```
Tracing expression #2
Cross x:2              y:20
```

An algebraic solution to this problem is obtained by equating the time-distance formulae for Carl and Alois and solving the resulting equation:

❑ [A]uthor d_carl(t)=d_alois(t) [↵]

   so[L]ve [↵]

```
#1:  D_CARL(t) := 10·t

#2:  D_ALOIS(t) := 10 + 5·t

#3:  D_CARL(t) = D_ALOIS(t)

#4:  t = 2
```

The solution (expression #4) gives the time of the overtaking, namely 2 seconds after the start. By evaluating one of the time-distance formulae at the 2 second mark we find the place where it occurs:

❑ [A]uthor d_carl(2) = [↵]

```
#5:  D_CARL(2) = 20
```

Now the student is confronted with the following thought experiment:

> "Carl will never overtake Alois: after 1 second Carl arrives at the point from which Alois started, i.e., at the 10 metre mark. In this second, however, Alois has run 5 metres, and is now at the 15 metre mark. Carl needs a further half second to reach this mark. But in this half second Alois has run a further 2.5 metres and is at the 17.5 metre mark. Carl needs a quarter second to reach this point, but in this time Alois has reached the 18.75 metre mark ... Regardless of how long one carries on this discussion, Alois is always ahead by a fraction."

Furthermore:

> "As the above calculation and common experience demonstrate, Carl overtakes Alois. Thus in the thought experiment above there must be an error. Find it."

One of the sections in Chapter 4 is a continuation of this example, under the title "Introduction to Limits".

New subjects

The first step in the problem-solving cycle is the choice of a model. One can only choose an appropriate model if one is familiar with enough possible candidates.

The third step in the problem-solving cycle is the solution of the model problem through calculation, i.e., with one or more algorithms that are associated with the model in use. Also in this case, one can only choose the right algorithms when one is familiar with enough different examples. It is not important here whether the algorithm is applied oneself or the performance of the algorithm is delegated to a computer. Even with DERIVE the student has to know, for example, that an equation is to be solved. (Here the model would be "equations" and the chosen algorithm would be "solution of equations".) This observation leads to a rather interesting point of view for mathematics: every mathematical (teaching-)subject can be located on a coordinate system with the following three axes:

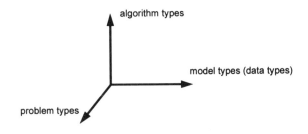

For instance the subject of *Newtonian Approximation* has the problem type coordinate of "approximate solution", the algorithm type of "Newton's Method" and the model type coordinate of "equation in one variable". The subject of *Multidimensional Newton's Method* has the same problem type and algorithm coordinates, but the model type coordinate is "systems of equations in many variables". One could also say: the model type determines *what* is worked on, the algorithm type determines *how* it is to be worked on, and the problem type determines *why* it is worked on.

The advantage of this method is the avoidance of repeating (both teaching and learning) work. For example, division is a type of algorithm that can be taught once but used more often, both for the model/data type "whole numbers" as well as for the model/data type "polynomials". Both algorithms, presently taught separately and quite differently, use the same principles and the same basic algorithm. It would be a rather rewarding and educational enterprise to compare the two algorithms even in contemporary courses. The problem type "decomposition into smallest parts" is dealt with once for "whole numbers" (here it is called "prime factorisation") and once for "polynomials" (where it is called "decomposition into linear factors"). Once an understanding for these cross-subject similarities exists, one can restrict oneself to rather few problem, data and algorithm types and nevertheless cover a great deal of mathematics. The demonstration of the interconnections would also help to show the beauty of mathematics as a whole.

The point of view explained above, to the best knowledge of the author, originates with Prof. Bruno Buchberger at RISC-Linz/Hagenberg, Austria.

A decent mathematical education should thus cover the most important models, the respectively important calculation methods and the most commonly seen problems that can be dealt with using these models.

In an effort to construct a new vision of mathematics instruction one should endeavour to expand the repertoire of models, calculation methods and problems. In the following we propose several ideas for new subjects.

Simplification of expressions: Simplification is simultaneously part of the most important and the most difficult parts of mathematics. Let's look at a few examples from my book *"Mathematics on the PC - Introduction to DERIVE"*.

❏ Simplify the expressions $1+2$, $1 \cdot x + 0$, $(x-1)(x+1)-x^2$, $\sqrt{4-2\sqrt{3}}$. Use the trailing equals sign to force an automatic application of the ›Simplify‹ command, e.g. [A]uthor $1+2=$ [↵]

```
#1:   1 + 2 = 3

#2:   1·x + 0 = x

                 2
#3:   (x - 1)·(x + 1) - x  = -1

#4:   √(4 - 2·√3) = √3 - 1
```

The first two examples are trivial, the third can easily be followed while the fourth requires a little more effort. In all four examples it is obvious that the expression to the right is simpler than the original expression on the left.

Through simplification an expression may (or should) change its outer appearance, but not its meaning. As well as the ›Simplify‹ command, both the ›Factor‹ and ›Expand‹ commands perform this.

❏ Apply both [S]implify and [F]actor to the expression $x(x(x-2)-5)+6$.

```
#5:   x·(x·(x - 2) - 5) + 6

         3     2
#6:   x  - 2·x  - 5·x + 6

#7:   (x - 1)·(x + 2)·(x - 3)
```

"Which of these three representations is the simplest?". The answer to this question has to be "In what sense simple?". It depends completely upon what is wanted from the simplified version.

- If one wants the version with the least number of characters, then expression #6 is the simplest.
- If one wants to determine the zeroes, then expression #7 is the simplest, since we can simply read them off the expression.
- If one wants to evaluate the polynomial with a calculator (one with only addition, multiplication and division) then expression #5 is the simplest, because we can evaluate without having to store intermediate results.

In a particular example the definition of simplest is also a part of the posing of the problem. In the sense of the above given coordinate system, we can talk about various problem types that all fall under "simplification". The phrase "bring to its simplest form", found in many if not all school mathematics textbooks, is a rather unclear expression which should be avoided.

A further aspect of simplification centres on correctness. Many apparently valid transformations are, when viewed more closely, invalid. A few examples:

Is $\sqrt{xy} = \sqrt{x}\sqrt{y}$ valid?   No, with $x = -1$, $y = -1$ this gives $1 = -1$.

Is $\arctan(\tan\theta) = \theta$ valid?   No, with $\theta = \pi$ this gives $0 = \pi$.

Is $\sqrt{\dfrac{1}{x}} = \dfrac{1}{\sqrt{x}}$ valid?   No, with $x = -1$ this gives $i = -i$.

Is $\ln(x^2) = 2\ln(x)$ valid?   No, with $x = -1$ this gives $0 = \dfrac{i\pi}{2}$.

An exercise based upon this idea involves the teacher giving various transformations or equivalences, and the students finding counter-examples, i.e., values for the variables where the equivalences do not hold. If one uses the computer, in the sense of the Scaffolding, to simplify the expressions, then the student can concentrate upon the appropriate choice of values, avoiding calculation errors and blockage-through-lack-of-knowledge (which easily occurs with, e.g., complex numbers).

❏ A̅uthor √(xy) =√x√y ⏎

    M̅anage S̅ubstitute ⏎ x: -1 ⏎ y: -1 ⏎

    S̅implify ⏎

```
#1:  √(x·y) = √x·√y
#2:  √((-1)·(-1)) = √(-1)·√(-1)
#3:  1 = -1
```

Another exercise is to reformulate a particular expression into a desired form using the computer. As an example, we simplify $\sqrt{xy} - \sqrt{x}\sqrt{y}$ to zero, which, as we saw above, is initially not possible with DERIVE.

❏ A̅uthor √(xy) -√x√y ⏎

    S̅implify ⏎

```
#4:  √(x·y) - √x·√y
#5:  √(x·y) - √x·√y
```

Now one uses the ›Declare‹ command to restrict the range of the variables appropriately, then we simplify again.

❏   [D]eclare [V]ariable x [↵]   [R]eal nonne[G]ative

[S]implify #4 [↵]

```
#6:   x :∈ Real [0, ∞)
#7:   0
```

In this example it is sufficient to restrict just one of the variables, for example x, to be non-negative. The students should attempt to have the equivalence work with the smallest possible amount of restriction.

A good study of such examples should provoke many "Aha!" experiences in the students. One learns much about the validity of transformations here. In comparison with all other commercial computer algebra systems, DERIVE is the most powerful and most accurate in this respect.

Equivalence of expressions: Two students solve the same problem and come up with different answers. Did one miscalculate? Not necessarily! A student solves an exercise with DERIVE from the schoolbook, but her answer differs from that in the solution manual. Did DERIVE make an error, or is the answer in the book wrong? Probably neither one nor the other. In both cases we are probably dealing with equivalent expressions, i.e., with expressions that appear different, but have the same meaning. Students should be aware of this possibility and know about the following two methods.

If one wants to determine whether two expressions are equivalent, then one simplifies their difference. If the answer is zero, then the two expressions are equivalent. If not, this is no proof that they are not equivalent. (There are proven results that for certain classes of formulae it is principally impossible to give an algorithm that determines whether an expression is equal to zero.) The problem of whether expressions are equivalent is closely related to the problem of simplifying expressions.

A second method to determine whether two expressions are equivalent is based on the knowledge that two expressions are equivalent if and only if they give the same result for all possible replacements of variables. From this we obtain the following "experimental" method: "replace all variables with arbitrary values (special values such as $0, 1$, $\pi/2$ and π should be avoided) and calculate the (decimal) values of the two expressions." If the results are different, then the expressions are definitely different. If the results agree, then one repeats the experiment with new values. When the expressions agree at more values, then the probability that the expressions agree is larger. (In this sense this probability after just the first experiment is very large.) The equivalence is nevertheless not *proven* even after the thousandth experiment.

In practice one mixes the two methods and uses the computer as follows: First one constructs the difference between the two expressions, and applies the ›Simplify‹ command. If after a reasonable time a zero is returned, then we know that the expressions are equivalent. If the answer is not zero, or the simplification takes too long (in DERIVE one can interrupt a calculation with ⌈ESC⌉ at any time), then one takes random values for the variables in the expression (most simply in the result from the difference calculation above) and applies the ›approX‹ command. If the result is far enough from zero, then we know that the expressions are not equivalent. If the result is zero, or something very close to zero (e.g. 3.456×10^{-12}), then one tries a second experiment with new values. In the event that (almost) zero appears again, then one can be practically certain that the expressions are equivalent.

Estimation: An oft-stated problem with the use of calculators is that students (and not only students) rely blindly on results from the machine. It is simple for typing mistakes to cause small errors that expand into large errors, even variations in the order of magnitude of a result: from the correct 123.4 it is easy to jump to the often not recognised as false value of 12340.0.

To counter this often-observed state of affairs we need to revive a skill important in the age of the slide-rule, namely the estimation of results. A student need not be able to calculate 4.981×21.734 by hand, but he should be able to make the approximation "about 5 times 20, thus about 100". Similarly the student should know that no trigonometric functions should appear in a polynomial.

Numerical approximation: A computer typically uses floating point numbers. Since only a finite number of decimal places can be stored and worked with, but most values have a finite number of decimal places (e.g. $1/3 = 0.3333333333333...$, $\pi = 3.1415926535897626...$), the lost decimal places lead to systematic errors.

These errors, known as rounding errors, often proliferate until they overwhelm a calculation. A rather dramatic example is the technically named "catastrophic cancellation", which occurs when two nearly exact values are subtracted. In the following examples we show how this appears with five digit precision. The effect appears, however, with any precision.

The difference between $a = 0.33333333$ and $b = 0.33334999$ is $d = 0.00001666$. With five significant digit floating point arithmetic, where everything after the fifth decimal place is simply cut off, we obtain the approximations $a' = 0.33333$ and $b' = 0.33334$. The difference is then $d' = 0.00001$. While the relative error between a and a' is only about 0.001% and the error between b and b' only around 0.003%, the relative error between d and d' is a huge 40%! This is because a' and b' both have five significant digits, while d' now has only one.

DERIVE's ability to work with arbitrary precision floating point numbers makes it an ideal tool to investigate this rather important but tricky subject. We look at three examples, the first and last from my book *"Mathematics on the PC - Introduction to DERIVE"*. There is a complete chapter in that book dealing with the subject of calculations using decimals and the associated problems that arise.

In the first example we replace the single variable in an expression with a value and evaluate it with differing accuracies.

❑   Enter $x\sqrt{x}\left(\sqrt{x+1} + \sqrt{x-1} - 2\sqrt{x}\right)$.

    Replace x with one million using Ⓜanage Ⓢubstitute.

    Ⓐuthor approx(#2) ⏎

    Ⓢimplify ⏎

```
#1:   x·√x·(√(x + 1) + √(x - 1) - 2·√x)

#2:   1000000·√1000000·(√(1000000 + 1) + √(1000000 - 1) - 2·√1000000)

#3:   APPROX(1000000·√1000000·(√(1000000 + 1) + √(1000000 - 1) - 2·√1000000))

#4:   0
```

With the default six digit precision the result is zero.

❑   Ⓐuthor approx(#2,15) ⏎

    Ⓢimplify ⏎

```
#5:   APPROX(1000000·√1000000·(√(1000000 + 1) + √(1000000 - 1) - 2·√1000000), 15)

#6:   -0.250012501243889
```

With fifteen significant digits the result is around $-1/4$, thus essentially non-zero. From this we get the questions: How can we guarantee that we get a good result? When can we trust the computer?

In the next example we solve an equation and then substitute one of the found solutions back in.

❏ Enter the polynomial $3x^4 - 420x^3 + 17900x^2 + 56000x - 1960000$.

so⃞L⃞ve ⃞↵⃞

```
      4       3        2
#7:  3·x  - 420·x  + 17900·x  + 56000·x - 1960000

#8:  x = 10

           ┌ 1415000    14000·√10091 ┐1/3   ┌ 14000·√10091              1415000 ┐1/3
#9:  x = - │ ─────── - ──────────── │    - │ ──────────── +          ─────── │    + -
           └   27            27      ┘      └      27                      27   ┘

           ┌ 176875    1750·√10091 ┐1/3   ┌ 1750·√10091    176875 ┐1/3   130
#10: x = │ ────── - ─────────── │    + │ ─────────── + ────── │    + ───  +
           └   27          27     ┘      └     27           27   ┘       3

           ┌ 176875    1750·√10091 ┐1/3   ┌ 1750·√10091    176875 ┐1/3   130
#11: x = │ ────── - ─────────── │    + │ ─────────── + ────── │    + ───  +
           └   27          27     ┘      └     27           27   ┘       3
```

Three of the solutions appear truncated on the screen. Expressions #8 and #9 are real, #10 and #11 are complex.

❏ Substitute expression #9 into the equation #7 using ⃞M⃞anage ⃞S⃞ubstitute.

appro⃞X⃞ ⃞↵⃞

```
          ┌   ┌ 1415000    14000·√10091 ┐1/3   ┌ 14000·√10091    1415000 ┐1/3     1
#12: 3·│ - │ ─────── - ──────────── │    - │ ──────────── + ─────── │    + ─
          └   └   27            27     ┘      └      27           27   ┘

#13: 68.1512
```

With the default six digit precision the evaluation gives an answer that is far from the known correct result of zero. Only an evaluation with 10 or 15 digits precision gives a result that lies near its proper value, i.e., zero:

❏ ⃞A⃞uthor approx(#12,10) ⃞↵⃞

⃞S⃞implify ⃞↵⃞

```
            ┌   ┌ 1415000    14000·√10091 ┐1/3   ┌ 14000·√10091    1415000 ┐1
#14: APPROX│ 3·│ - │ ─────── - ──────────── │    - │ ──────────── + ─────── │
            └   └   └   27            27     ┘      └      27           27   ┘

                   -4
#15: - 2.300213519·10
```

❏ ⃞A⃞uthor approx(#12,15) ⃞↵⃞

⃞S⃞implify ⃞↵⃞

```
            ┌   ┌ 1415000    14000·√10091 ┐1/3   ┌ 14000·√10091    1415000 ┐1
#16: APPROX│ 3·│ - │ ─────── - ──────────── │    - │ ──────────── + ─────── │
            └   └   └   27            27     ┘      └      27           27   ┘

                      -10
#17: - 9.28239400018945·10
```

The third and last example shows how rounding errors can become visible when plotting a graph.

❑ Enter the expression $\dfrac{x^2-1}{x+1}+\dfrac{1}{3}$ and plot it. Set the graphics window precision:

[O]ptions [A]ccuracy 9 [↵]

On close inspection (see the left picture below) one sees a small hole around the coordinates $(-1,-5/3)$. This arises because the expression is not defined at this point and has a so-called *removable singularity* there.

❑ Zoom in around the point $(-1,-5/3)$ until the right-hand picture appears.

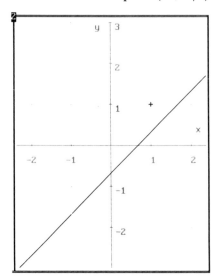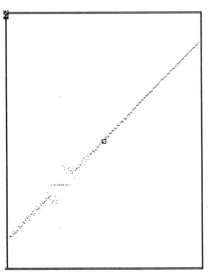

As the axis scale approaches the precision of the graphics window, the graph seems to dissolve around the removable singularity. The reason here is the occurrence of rounding errors. These occur since the denominator is very small around the value $x=-1$. Division by a small number is equivalent to multiplication by a large number, which massively enlarges the rounding error in the numerator and makes it significant, here graphically.

All the above examples would be impossible to carry out by hand calculation or with a standard calculator.

Further in this direction we can teach models that, due to time constraints, have no space in current mathematics, e.g., matrices, discrete mathematics, multidimensional analysis or chaos theory.

New teaching methods

"Children are using computers up to five hours per day, almost as much time as is spent in school" proclaims a specialist journal from 1994. With the assistance of computer games such as SIM CITY (almost 2 million copies sold in four years) children are learning about interconnected economic, social and ecological systems. Edutainment (from ›EDUcation‹ and ›enterTAINMENT‹) is the catchword bantered around by education experts. The computer makes it possible!

The computer can also help add a little more zest and eagerness to learn to mathematics education. In an Austrian study over several years it was found that those schools that regularly used DERIVE experienced more self-directed study, independence and communication about mathematics than in those control group schools where DERIVE was not used.

Computers and software however are not enough. The way in which they are used is the key. New methods are possible with computer support. One of these methods was introduced in Chapter 2, the Scaffolding. Here we sketch further details to form a more complete picture.

Mathematics is something that has grown over millennia. One of the oldest areas of mathematics is geometry, with roots that reach back into Babylonian and Etruscan times, around 3000 BC. The Egyptians, who due to the annual flooding of the Nile had to resurvey the land regularly, developed a powerful empirical science from the Babylonian beginnings. All the formulae and rules known to the Egyptians (including Pythagorus' Theorem and the formula for the volume of a truncated pyramid) were found using the trial and error method. Shortly before the beginning of the Common Era the Greeks took to the mathematical stage: they used the deductive methods of their philosophy on the geometrical and numerical knowledge of the Egyptians and established mathematics as we know it today: a deductive science in which logic, definitions, theorems and proofs play the major roles. Over the two millennia since then this core of mathematics has increased in detail and size, and has taken on many subjects in addition to the original ones.

Milestones in recent times include algebra from the Arabs, the calculus of infinitesimals from Leibnitz and Newton and analytic geometry from Descartes.

The genetic principle: Many things in nature grow by replaying the entire developmental history of its gene-line in fast-forward. The human embryo is the most well known example. Starting as a single cell it goes through generations of cell division, becoming an ever more self-organised and differentiated cell-complex. While at the beginning the cell can do everything it needs itself (this is the feature of simple single-celled life) after some divisions the cells begin to specialise (this is the feature of higher, multi-celled lifeforms) and the embryo differentiates more and more body parts. In an early stage the embryo passes through a fish phase, it has gills that later develop into lungs. The fish phase is followed by the reptile phase. Mammalian features are only recognisable in the last stages of development. Millions of years of evolution, from the start of single-celled life up to Homo Sapiens, is played back in nine months of pregnancy: a wonder of nature and a perfect example of a very powerful natural principle.

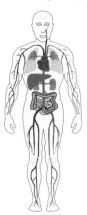

This genetic principle should guide us in our teaching methods: instead of designing a modern, extremely logical approach to a mathematical concept and drumming it into the students' heads, it might be more appropriate to follow the historical development of the subject at hand. In this task the computer is a rather useful tool: properly used it makes it possible for a concept that has been developed over centuries to be presented in a few hours of teaching in such a way that students can follow the development of the idea and come to understand it well.

The short outline of mathematical history above has shown one thing clearly: during the first half of the 5000-odd years that mathematics has existed, experiments were the only source of mathematical knowledge. From this observation, considering the genetic principle above, we derive two recommendations:

- In the early school years an *experimental* mathematics should be in the foreground.
- At every stage of schooling the introduction of a new subject should be accompanied by an *experimental phase*.

For example with the help of questions like, "How many zeroes does 100! have?", which could be answered after extensive experimentation, a student could obtain a deep understanding of divisibility.

The **classroom situation** can be altered through the use of computers. To date, we have almost exclusively used *front teaching*, where the teacher is active and the students passive. The opposite of this would be *surround teaching*, where the students work at a computer either freely experimenting or under the guidance of the teacher, while the teacher acts as an advisor and assistant in case of trouble. Such teaching situations where the students are active and the teacher (principally) passive, especially encourage the independent activity of the students.

A third variation is *Partnership*, where (ideally two) students work together. Here it

is possible for two equally gifted students to encourage each other, or to have more gifted students help those less gifted. Not only in the first instance, but also in the second, both students profit: the less gifted student receives support, while the more gifted student learns through teaching. The partnership also works on improving communication skills (and not only regarding mathematics).

The perfect teaching methodology lies in a good mixture of these three forms.

Examinations: Finally something will have to change, and will change, with examinations. Ideally an examination should be able to be completed with very few tools of any kind, for the following reasons:

- It should not be the purpose of mathematics teaching to test how well a student can use a tool. This skill should be demanded only at the most minimal level.
- Social justice must exist. It should not matter whether a student can afford a more expensive (and thus better) tool than his classmates with less well-off parents. Forbidding certain tools is not always the solution to this problem since no-one can guarantee that this ban will be enforceable. Already today a teacher needs to be a specialist to differentiate between allowed and disallowed calculators.

- Something that a machine can do better and faster than a person should not be in the foreground of determining the mathematical abilities of a student. Correct simplification, differentiation, integration, plotting, etc. should not be an important part of the tested mathematical skills.

Instead of requiring a graph plot, now just a single keypress with the correct tool, the graph could be simply given and the student no longer needs the (probably expensive) tool. For an examination a computer or calculator should perform the role that a dictionary plays in a foreign language examination, acting simply as a "crutch".

A high point of future mathematics and a proper teaching-oriented innovation would be examinations that were based around skills like problem-solving or conceptual understanding of the subject, i.e., on something other than machine-like calculation skills.

What must a Mathematician be capable of? - New old educational goals

As a language course must give a basic command of the language in question, a mathematics course must provide some basic command of mathematical concepts and ideas. An indispensable aspect of this is the training of those properties that make a person a mathematician. In the following we list several of these capabilities and suggest some examples that are appropriate for teaching: some of which need a computer, many of which do not. Thus, as said before, the ideal mathematics course of the future will rely only occasionally on computers!

This section has been given the subtitle "New old educational goals" because those aspects of mathematics that are necessary parts of every mathematical skill were once the core of mathematics teaching. Mathematics, due to the goals that we describe below, was a central part of the study of philosophy: mathematics was body-building for the mind.

The goals described here have high practical relevance for all people, not only mathematicians. With these goals mathematics teaching will prove its social relevance; successful students in mathematics will make better doctors, business managers, lawyers, etc.

Understanding

Understanding is the principal characteristic and ability of a mathematician. By understanding we mean the exact interpretation of a text. Since a text can have multiple meanings or even be contradictory, comprehension requires the ability to recognise plurality of meaning or contradiction and, where necessary, to look into each possible interpretation. As simple as it usually is to understand a short sentence, a longer sentence can be almost incomprehensible, for example the instructions for a video recorder, an insurance policy, a law statute or the text exercises in a mathematics book.

While we are on the subject: text exercises can and should be used for practising and training understanding skills. But these are some of the most complex such examples. A problem in logic is to work with texts that are composed from very few symbols. These texts are mathematical formulae. Formulae are one of the easiest ways to practice understanding. When using them the teacher can control the amount of complexity, ambiguity, etc. present. A simple problem to practice understanding is to translate the meaning of a formula into everyday language, e.g.,

- $\forall x \left(x^2 \geq 0 \right)$ ... The square of a number is non-negative.
- $\exists y \left(y^2 = 4 \right)$ ... There is a number with its square equal to 4.

A valuable and quite useful practice in this age is the understanding of expert opinions. What does it mean when an expert says, "There is no proof of environmental damage caused by this installation"? It does not mean that it is clean (even if the manager of the facility wants to interpret it this way). Neither does it mean that the installation is dangerous (even if the protesters want to interpret it that way). For this exercise every daily newspaper is full of examples waiting to be used.

Description

The dual of understanding is description. It is based upon constructing a text with a certain given meaning. Ideally the text should be so formulated that it is unambiguous and easily read by another person. This is an important skill not only for every student of mathematics; it is indispensable for every teacher too.

Here is another example where working with mathematical formulae is an excellent training instrument, only this time we work in the opposite direction: a given mathematical fact should be written as a formula (i.e., it should be *formulated*), e.g.,

- 27 is divisible by 3 ... $\exists t(27 = t \cdot 3)$.
- Every number is greater than its predecessor ... $\forall x(x > x - 1)$.

In the process it should be made clear how important it is to define the abbreviated terms that are used, and to define from the outset the language and methods that are being used.

- Every number divides itself, $\forall x(divides(x,x))$, where $divides(t,p){:}\Leftrightarrow \exists v(t \cdot v = p)$.

In every newspaper there are numerous examples that can also be used to practice description skills. After a text has been understood - see above - a new formulation can be sought that is shorter, clearer, less ambiguous, etc.

From these first two educational goals one sees that logic should take a place in mathematics. While mathematics talks *with* formulae, i.e., it uses formulae to talk about mathematical ideas, logic talks *about* formulae, i.e., the formulae are themselves the objects of investigation. DERIVE's ability to work with logical expressions and to evaluate truth tables can be rather helpful here.

```
#1:  x < 1 AND x > 2

#2:  false

#3:  x > 1 OR x > 2

#4:  x > 1

#5:  TRUTH_TABLE(x, y, x AND y, x IMP y, x OR NOT x)
```

	x	y	x AND y	x IMP y	x OR NOT x
	true	true	true	true	true
#6:	true	false	false	false	true
	false	true	false	true	true
	false	false	false	true	true

Argumentation

Argumentation is about finding convincing reasons for something. In order that they are convincing, they must, amongst other things, be consistent with the state of knowledge of the listener. For instance the arguments about the necessity of a certain medical therapy are different if the doctor is talking to a medical colleague rather than to the distressed, uneducated father of the child.

Argumentation connects almost seamlessly with the ability to describe. While description is "only" the finding of a suitable formulation for a given content, in argumentation the content must first be found.

Argumentation is the first step towards the very important mathematical skill of constructing proofs. Exercises of the following sort serve to train this skill and should take more and more importance in the exercise and examination system:

- Explain why one uses the first derivative to find the extreme values of a function.
- If a curve is symmetric in both the x- and y-axes, is it then symmetric through the origin? Give the reason or find a counter-example.

The important understanding that even a thousand examples are not proof of a statement, while one counterexample is enough to disprove it, should be developed through various case studies.

Furthermore the danger of accepting an argument too quickly should be demonstrated. Helmut Heugl of Vienna has provided the following rather illustrative and, for educational purposes, quite useful example:

- A square has sides of length 1. Thus the sum of the lengths of the upper and right hand sides is 2. Making a single step, as shown below in the second picture from the left, does not change the total length, the resulting step thus has also length 2. Cutting further steps as shown in the third and further pictures below does not change the total length, so we see that all such steps have length 2. If we proceed then the limiting case is the diagonal, which must, therefore, have length 2. Since we already know that the diagonal has length $\sqrt{2}$, we deduce that $2 = \sqrt{2}$ ...

Recreational mathematics books are full of such examples. We need only the courage to introduce them to normal teaching situations. Mathematics would, especially in the eyes of many of the students, lose much of its unappetising dryness.

To be critical

Our world-view is generated from all the information that we receive over the years. What we learn in school, what we read in books and, to an ever-increasing extent, what we receive through the various media, forms our view of the world. Much of this information is (purposely or not) false. A naive lack of criticism leads to gullibility or even loss of contact with reality.

Instead of simply absorbing information, we need to apply a *plausibility check* beforehand: could that which we are being told actually be true? Another aspect of this, for example, appropriate to the times we receive a chain letter, is a *reality check*: can what is described here even work?

A healthy scepticism towards information of all sorts, in particular information that is intended to generate belief, is the basis of responsibility. This scepticism makes it possible to make rational decisions, for example when voting or in referenda.

- An example of the plausibility check: history teaches us that the Cheops Pyramid, consisting of more than two million stones with an average weight of around 2.5 tonnes, was built in twenty years. Can this even be possible? Two million stones in 20 years makes 100,000 stones per year. If we assume that the pyramid was built year-round (while it is more probable that the full workforce was only available during the annual flooding of the Nile), then this means 275 stones per day. Assuming 12 working hours per day (more is improbable due to both the scarcity of wood and the horrendous amount of smoke that would have been generated if fires where lit for night work) we derive that this was 23 stones per hour or equivalently a stone every 2.6 minutes. Every 2.6 minutes a stone cut from a quarry, a stone arriving at the Nile, a stone transported upstream, a stone being transported to the site and a stone being placed with millimetre accuracy. This would not even be possible with modern technology! Even with very many workers this cannot be believed: today, with computer assistance, a building site with one hundred thousand or more workers is unmanageable. It must have been different. Any theory that suggests that the Cheops Pyramid was started before Cheops' time should be investigated.

• An example of a reality check: If someone had invested a penny at five per cent interest in the year 1 A.D., then in 1995 it would have a value of 17,800 billion billion billion pounds (= $£1.78 \times 10^{40}$). With today's gold price that would mean 44.9 million solid gold balls the size of the Earth. This sum is not only way beyond our powers of imagination, it surpasses everything of any worth on this planet and thus demonstrates that an interest system such as that in use today cannot be maintained or even conceived of over longer time spans (i.e., over centuries).

Similar examples can be found in almost all areas of study. Here we see unexpected possibilities for interdisciplinary teaching arise. We cannot, however, let the critical attitude get out of hand. A reasonable middle should be the goal of a good mathematical education.

Understanding numbers, percentages and orders of magnitude

This point ties in closely with the preceding points. Recall the number from the last example: $£1.78 \times 10^{40}$. Is such a quantity of money even imaginable?

When the national budget or trade deficit is talked about on television, it is done so in units of thousands of millions of pounds. For most people the possibility of visualising a number peaks at about 100,000, the number of people who can fill a (rather large) soccer stadium. We cannot visualise larger numbers because we do not have any tangible comparisons. There is no real (subjective) difference between a million and a thousand million. Who cares about a few millions in the treasury?

It should be a task of mathematics education to teach methods to make numbers plausible, for instance to reduce the national budget to a per capita value, converting money into gold balls, lining up products in rows so long that they go several times around the planet, etc.

• Austria is attempting to limit the national budget deficit to 100 thousand million ATS. The number becomes tangible only when we share it out amongst the population. Spread amongst the 7 million Austrians, the amount is around

14,286 ATS per person, including all children, students and pensioners. For a four person family that makes their part of Austria's new debt around 60,000 ATS (around £4000), approximately the cost of a second-hand car (or a very expensive holiday!). And this for each and every Austrian!

A few examples of numbers that can be used for comparison.

- The largest number in nature is 10^{80}. It is the number of neutrons in the universe.
- The estimated diameter of the universe is 7×10^{26} metres.
- The estimated age of the universe is 15 thousand million years, that is, 4.73×10^{17} seconds.
- The approximate weight of Earth is 10^{24} kilograms, that of the Sun is 10^{30}.
- The number of haemoglobin molecules in the human body is around 6×10^{21}.

Another general problem of numeracy is percentages. The difference between relative and absolute values on one hand, and the understanding of relative values on the other, requires an appropriate education. This should be one of the goals of general mathematics teaching. The following example is due to Helmut Heugl:

- In the news it is claimed that the Consumer Price Index increased 4.5% in the previous month. How believable is this figure? It must first be asked how this number is even calculated. This is done by calculating the price of a so-called "basket of goods" that consists of various commodities needed for day to day living. If the basket cost £975 last year, and now costs £1000, then the CPI increase is indeed 4.5%. If one however allows an error in the basket price of just 2% (that's a difference of just £20 over the £1000), then the CPI increase could be anywhere between 2.4 and 6.6%. With a purchaser error of 5%, the range goes from a deflation of 0.7% up to 9.7% inflation. The value or worth (i.e. exactness) of this inflation rate thus depends massively upon the chances accompanying the test purchase, e.g., which shops are visited. When one notes that politicians often make a great fuss about a difference of a few tenths of a percentage, one realises that we are often fed a lot of hogwash because of our non-understanding of percentages.

Examples of this are to be found daily in newspapers. Discussing them opens whole new vistas for the teacher.

Abstraction

By abstraction we mean the reduction of something to its necessary features. The art of abstraction is to get by with the least possible number of features. Thus one restricts oneself to those features that are most characteristic for the object in question. The following picture is immediately recognisable as a human face even though it consists of only five simple elements.

The face remains, however, anonymous. The masters of abstraction are the caricaturists: they can capture a face unmistakably in a few strokes.

A practical example for abstraction are the so-called pictograms, which convey the same information irrespective of the language of the land. Modern travel would not be possible without them.

In the following we give various exercises for the training of the ability to abstract:

- Concept-guessing using drawing: one student attempts to convey a concept to a fellow student using only drawn symbols.
- Concept-guessing using example: one student attempts to communicate a concept to a fellow student using only his body, somewhat like the party game "Charades".

Both exercises can be made into rather entertaining games, in that one organises the students into groups that compete to communicate a concept in the least possible amount of time. Mathematics teaching can (and should!) sometimes be playful. Joy in learning is possible!

- Describe a characteristic property: one student attempts to describe a given (general) object by its properties. The other students play against her by trying to find (a) things that satisfy the properties but are not the desired object, or (b) things that are an example of the type of object without being described by the properties. Through this game the student is forced to present a new collection of properties. An example using the object "Bottle" might start as follows:

Student: A bottle is a container with an opening.

Other student: This glass is not a bottle.

Student: A bottle is a container that tapers to a hole at the top.

And so on.

All exercises where an object is sought that satisfies certain properties help in the schooling of the ability to abstract. With exercises like the following the graphics component of a computer algebra system is of great help:

• Find a term t whose graph looks like the following, e.g.:

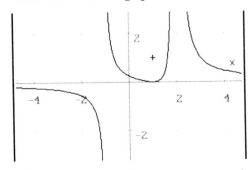

• Find a term   , so that $/$.
• Find a proper rational function   , so that
• Sketch all possible cases of the graph of a polynomial of order 4.

The ability to abstract is necessary for the solution of problems. In the process of translating a real problem into a model problem, the ability to abstract is of great help. On one hand the model problem will be simpler the fewer properties of the original problem are incorporated into it, on the other hand there must be enough of the original properties to allow a solution to be found. The last part is often very difficult to decide and often leads to repetitions of the problem solving cycle: for instance when the solar heating of the interior of a car is significant, then even the colour of the car must be taken into a model.

Induction and Deduction

In the attempt to characterise a concept through its properties one uses a skill known as *induction*. Induction is the process of moving from various particular examples to a general rule, from the specific to the general. In the example above the student imagined various bottles and tried to discover the similarities.

The opposite of induction is *deduction*, which is where one applies a general rule to some special case, i.e., one moves from the general to the specific.

Induction and deduction are two important logical skills, so one can simply reach back for the established exercises in the subject. (The inclusion of logic in mathematics teaching was argued above.) The modern development of computer programming features both skills. The creation of a program is an inductive process: from the knowledge of how one solves concrete examples (e.g., how one sorts a list of numbers) one derives a general process for the task at hand that works for arbitrary input. The application of a program is a deductive process, where the general rules incorporated in the program are applied to the special case of a particular problem.

Good exercises for induction include:

- Development of algorithms.
- Thought Sports of the type: "what comes next in the series: 1 - 4 - 9 - 16 -"?

A good exercise for deduction is:

- Manually performing an algorithm.

A detailed example for the inductive process of programming is to be found in my book *"Mathematics on the PC - Introduction to DERIVE"*, where the development of a toolbox for analytic geometry is described in detail.

The examples presented in Chapter 2, equation solving and applied trigonometry, can be directly used for teaching purposes. The Scaffolding principle explained there is easily applied to other examples, where DERIVE is used as partly a teaching tool, partly as a trainer and partly as an extended calculator. It can take on other roles, as described in Chapter 3: it can serve as an experimental tool, and as a visualisation tool.

As one can see in the presently available literature, there are no limits to what can be envisioned for the application of computer algebra systems in teaching. In this chapter we present a number of examples that can be taken directly into practice, and should also act as stimulants for the development of other examples. Thus we have aimed for compact, easily understood and immediately emulable presentations. The first three examples originated with Peter Schüller of Vienna. Occasionally we will refer to methods and goals presented in Chapters 2 and 3.

Example 1: Curve fitting

Approximate the function $y = \dfrac{x^2 - 2}{7} - 3.3\sin(2x)$ through the points $x = 1.3 / 1.75 / 2.3 / 2.7 / 3.3 / 3.95 / 4.75$ with a polynomial of order 6. Calculate the polynomial and plot the curves of it and the original function. Derive the integral over the domain of approximation and thus determine the relative error of the fitted curve.

Owing to the way the problem is presented we opt for approximate calculations with 10 digit precision. We select approximate calculations since the problem uses decimal values in its presentation. We use 10 digit precision based upon the rule of thumb that one should use 3 or 4 digits more precision than the degree of the polynomial used for interpolation.

❏   ⬚Option ⬚Precision Mode: ⬚Approximate Digits: 10 ⬚↵

```
#1:  Precision := Approximate

#2:  PrecisionDigits := 10
```

We give the approximated function the name h, so that it is easily referred to in the process of solving the problem. The assignment can be done either with the ›Declare‹ command or with the ›Author‹ command. The second looks more comfortable.

❏   ⬚Author h(x):=(x^2-2)/7 - 3.3 sin(2x) ⬚↵

```
              2
             x  - 2
#3:  H(x) := ——————— - 3.3·SIN(2·x)
               7
```

The seven interpolation points are entered as a two column matrix, since the FIT function, used later to calculate the polynomial, requires this format for its second argument. To place the x-values in the first column and the corresponding function values in the second, we use the VECTOR function as follows:

❏   ⬚Author
         vector([x,h(x)],x,[1.3,1.75,2.3,2.7,3.3,3.95,4.75]) ⬚↵
         ⬚Simplify ⬚↵

```
#4:  VECTOR([x, H(x)], x, [1.3, 1.75, 2.3, 2.7, 3.3, 3.95, 4.75])

       ⎡ 1.3   -1.745440241 ⎤
       ⎢                     ⎥
       ⎢ 1.75   1.309370365  ⎥
       ⎢                     ⎥
       ⎢ 2.3    3.749180311  ⎥
       ⎢                     ⎥
#5:    ⎢ 2.7    3.305837094  ⎥
       ⎢                     ⎥
       ⎢ 3.3    0.2419135004 ⎥
       ⎢                     ⎥
       ⎢ 3.95  -1.353292142  ⎥
       ⎢                     ⎥
       ⎣ 4.75   3.185498697  ⎦
```

One can calculate arbitrary fitting curves with the FIT function. The only requirement is that the equations must be linear in the unknown coefficients. The desired polynomial of order 6 has the general form $ax^6 + bx^5 + cx^4 + dx^3 + ex^2 + fx + g$ and thus has seven undetermined coefficients. Since we also have seven points, we have the special case of an interpolation polynomial that will meet the approximated curve exactly at the seven selected points. In the following the matrix of points is referred to as #5.

❑ Author `fit([x,ax^6+bx^5+cx^4+dx^3+ex^2+fx+g],#5)` ↵

S implify ↵

$$\text{\#6:} \quad \text{FIT}\left[x, a \cdot x^6 + b \cdot x^5 + c \cdot x^4 + d \cdot x^3 + e \cdot x^2 + f \cdot x + g\right], \quad \begin{bmatrix} 1.3 & -1.745440241 \\ 1.75 & 1.309370365 \\ 2.3 & 3.749180311 \\ 2.7 & 3.305837094 \\ 3.3 & 0.2419135004 \\ 3.95 & -1.353292142 \\ 4.75 & 3.185498697 \end{bmatrix}$$

#7: $-0.1229035871 \cdot x^6 + 1.638354650 \cdot x^5 - 7.134566521 \cdot x^4 + 8.560539174 \cdot x^3 + 13.3$

Expression #7 is the desired interpolation polynomial. For the graphic comparison we first plot the seven points

❑ Open an adjacent graphics window with P lot B eside ↵

Plot the point matrix #5 with P lot ↵

Zoom out twice with F10 .

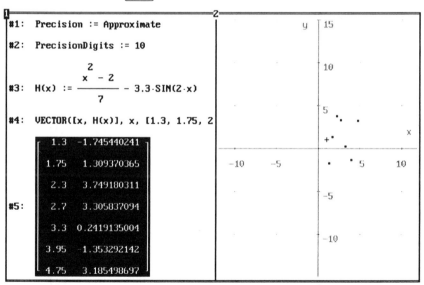

#1: Precision := Approximate

#2: PrecisionDigits := 10

#3: $H(x) := \dfrac{x^2 - 2}{7} - 3.3 \cdot \text{SIN}(2 \cdot x)$

#4: VECTOR([x, H(x)], x, [1.3, 1.75, 2

#5: $\begin{bmatrix} 1.3 & -1.745440241 \\ 1.75 & 1.309370365 \\ 2.3 & 3.749180311 \\ 2.7 & 3.305837094 \\ 3.3 & 0.2419135004 \\ 3.95 & -1.353292142 \\ 4.75 & 3.185498697 \end{bmatrix}$

Now the plot frame is restricted to the area of the seven points

❏ [R]ange [↵]

Select the four frame boundaries as shown in the left picture.

The right picture appears after pressing the [↵] key.

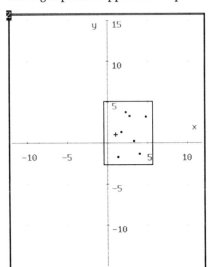
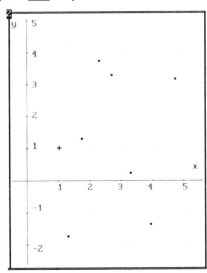

❏ Select and plot the interpolation polynomial, i.e. expression #7

Select and plot the original function *h*, i.e. expression #3.

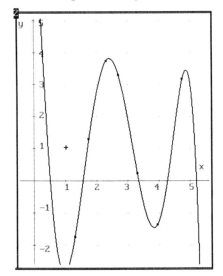
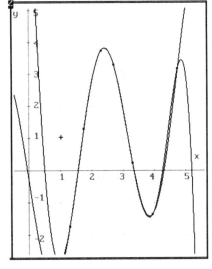

Now we need to calculate the integrals of the interpolation polynomial and the original function over the interval [1.3, 4.75] and thus determine the relative error.

To integrate we can either use the ›Calculus Integrate‹ command or the INT function directly. The four arguments for INT are: function, integration variable, lower integration limit, upper integration limit. If no limits of integration are given then the indefinite integral is calculated.

❑   Ⓐuthor   `int(h(x),x,1.3,4.75)`   ⏎

   Ⓢimplify   ⏎

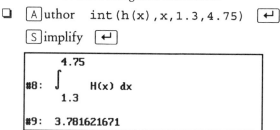

#8: $\int_{1.3}^{4.75} H(x)\,dx$

#9:   3.781621671

The integral of the interpolation polynomial is similarly derived.

❑   Ⓐuthor   `int(#7,x,1.3,4.75)`   ⏎

   Ⓢimplify   ⏎

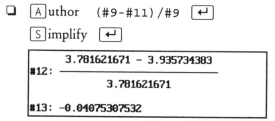

#10: $\int_{1.3}^{4.75} (-0.1229035871 \cdot x^6 + 1.638354650 \cdot x^5 - 7.134566521 \cdot x^4 + 8.560539174 \cdot x^3$

#11:   3.935734383

For a value y and an approximation $\tilde{y}$ the relative error is defined as $\dfrac{y - \tilde{y}}{y}$.

To determine the relative error of the integrals we proceed:

❑   Ⓐuthor   `(#9-#11)/#9`   ⏎

   Ⓢimplify   ⏎

#12: $\dfrac{3.781621671 - 3.935734383}{3.781621671}$

#13:   -0.04075307532

The combination of differences due to interpolation plus the effects of 10 digit precision leads to an error of approximately 4%, which could be reduced but not eradicated by using higher precision.

Before we go onto a further example, we should go back to exact precision and six digit calculation.

Example 2: Simulating two dice

The throwing of two dice is to be simulated. In the process the ideas of probability and frequency distributions should be compared and contrasted

The throw of a single die is easily simulated using the pseudo random number generator RANDOM.

❑ [A]uthor   dice:=1+random(6)   [↵]

[A]uthor   dice=   [↵]

[A]uthor   dice=   [↵]

[A]uthor   dice=   [↵]

```
#1:   dice := 1 + RANDOM(6)

#2:   dice = 1

#3:   dice = 1

#4:   dice = 4
```

Each simplification of the variable DICE results in the throw of a die. With the variable THROW we determine the sum of two dice:

❑ [A]uthor   throw:=dice+dice   [↵]

In order to simulate five throws of two dice, we simplify a vector containing five instances of the THROW variable. We can repeat this experiment.

❑ [A]uthor   [throw,throw,throw,throw,throw]   [↵]

[S]implify   [↵]

[S]implify #6   [↵]

```
#5:   throw := dice + dice

#6:   [throw, throw, throw, throw, throw]

#7:   [6, 8, 6, 6, 10]

#8:   [7, 8, 3, 6, 5]
```

In order to enter the number of throws as an argument, we define a function which we call THROWS.

❑ [A]uthor   throws(n):=vector(throw,i,1,n)   [↵]

[A]uthor   throws(20)   [↵]

[S]implify   [↵]

⬚ $\boxed{\text{S}}$implify #10 $\boxed{\leftarrow}$

```
#9:   THROWS(n) := VECTOR(throw, i, 1, n)

#10: THROWS(20)

#11: [7, 8, 8, 6, 8, 8, 10, 9, 7, 8, 9, 5, 12, 10, 5, 8, 10, 9, 9, 9]

#12: [3, 6, 4, 9, 7, 5, 6, 5, 7, 11, 7, 8, 6, 10, 9, 9, 9, 6, 6, 8]
```

We are interested in how often the possible values (2,3,4,...,11,12) occur in such an experiment. For teaching use, a function FREQUENCY should be prepared in advance, which can be simply loaded from a file that we will call EXAMPLE2.MTH. At the end of this example we give the definitions of this and other functions.

❑ $\boxed{\text{T}}$ransfer $\boxed{\text{L}}$oad $\boxed{\text{U}}$tility example2 $\boxed{\leftarrow}$

$\boxed{\text{A}}$uthor frequency(#12) $\boxed{\leftarrow}$

$\boxed{\text{S}}$implify $\boxed{\leftarrow}$ (results in expression #14 below)

Further frequency distributions for 20, 50 and 100 throws are to be calculated as follows:

❑ $\boxed{\text{A}}$uthor frequency(throws(20)) $\boxed{\leftarrow}$

$\boxed{\text{S}}$implify $\boxed{\leftarrow}$ (results in expression #16 below)

$\boxed{\text{A}}$uthor frequency(throws(50)) $\boxed{\leftarrow}$

$\boxed{\text{S}}$implify $\boxed{\leftarrow}$ (results in expression #18 below)

$\boxed{\text{A}}$uthor frequency(throws(100)) $\boxed{\leftarrow}$

$\boxed{\text{S}}$implify $\boxed{\leftarrow}$ (results in expression #20 below)

#14:			#16:			#18:			#20:	
2	0		2	3		2	2		2	2
3	1		3	0		3	3		3	4
4	1		4	1		4	5		4	8
5	2		5	0		5	2		5	12
6	5		6	4		6	6		6	17
7	3		7	3		7	13		7	17
8	2		8	7		8	8		8	14
9	4		9	1		9	2		9	7
10	1		10	1		10	6		10	8
11	1		11	0		11	2		11	8
12	0		12	0		12	1		12	3

In order to present these results graphically one proceeds as follows:

❑   Open an adjacent graphics window with the command ⎡P⎤lot ⎡B⎤eside ⎡↵⎤

To connect the points together, the graphics windows settings need to be changed as follows:

❑   ⎡O⎤ptions ⎡S⎤tate ⎡⇄⎤ Mode: ⎡C⎤onnected ⎡↵⎤

    Select and plot expression #14.

    Zoom out three times with the ⎡F10⎤ key.

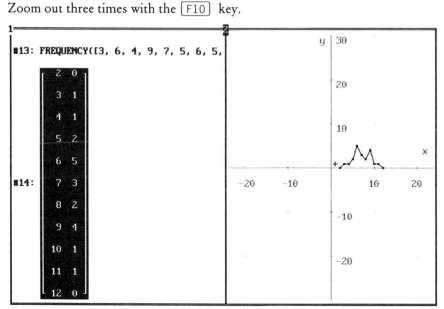

❑   Select and plot the other three frequency distributions, i.e. the expressions #16, #18 and #20.

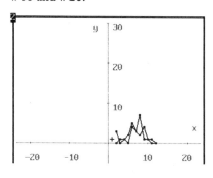
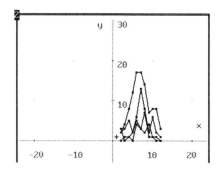

The absolute frequency distributions of experiments with varying numbers of throws are not comparable in this way. For this one needs the *relative* frequency distribution. This is calculated by norming the absolute frequency distribution, i.e. dividing the frequency by the total number of throws. The pre-programmed function RELFREQUENCY is so defined. Since the following results are interesting only as approximations, we do not need to use fractional calculations; two-digit accuracy suffices.

❑ [O]ption [P]recision Mode: [A]pproximate Digits: 2 [↵]

> #21: Precision := Approximate
>
> #22: PrecisionDigits := 2

Next we calculate the relative frequency of a new experiment with 20 throws.

❑ [A]uthor relfrequency(throws(20)) [↵]

[S]implify [↵]

Clear the previous graphs with [D]elete [A]ll [↵]

Plot the above-calculated matrix with the relative frequencies.

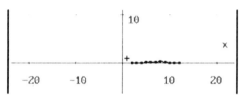

Since all y coordinates remain less that 1, independent of the number of throws, we should select a better plot frame.

❑ [R]ange ...choose boundaries as per the left picture[↵]

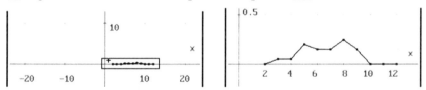

❑ Simplify the expression relfrequency(throws(20)) again and plot the resulting graph.

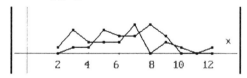

We compare the two relative frequency distributions with the corresponding probability distribution. This was saved in the file EXAMPLE2 under the name LIKELY.

❑ [A]uthor `likely` [↵]

Simplify this and plot the expression.

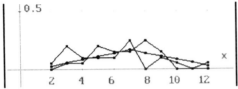

The differences are clear. Before we continue to calculate and plot the graphs with 50, 100 and 200 throws, we should clear the screen of all but the last probability distribution plot.

❑ [D]elete [B]utlast [↵]

[A]lgebra [A]uthor `relfrequency(throws(50))` [↵]

[S]implify [↵]

[P]lot [P]lot

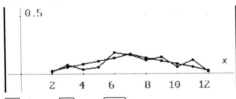

❑ [D]elete [L]ast [↵]

Repeat the above procedure for an experiment with 100 throws.

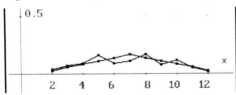

❑ Repeat the above procedure for an experiment with 200 throws.

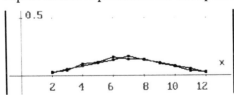

From a visual comparison of the pictures, it is clear that the relative frequency distribution comes closer to the probability distribution with more throws of the dice.

With the built in function AVERAGE one can calculate the statistical average. We apply it to experiments with 20 and 50 throws of the dice.

❏ 　[A]uthor　average(würfe(20))= 　[↵]

　　[A]uthor　average(würfe(50))= 　[↵]

```
#35: AVERAGE(THROWS(20)) = 7.4
#36: AVERAGE(THROWS(50)) = 7.2
```

How the statistical average moves closer to the probabilistic average will become clear through the following experiment. We calculate the average for 50, 100, 150, 200, 250, 300, 350, 400, 450 and 500 throws. For this we use the VECTOR function with start 50, end 500 and step 50.

❏ 　[A]uthor　vector([n,average(würfe(n))],n,50,500,50) 　[↵]

　　[S]implify 　[↵]

#38:

$$
\begin{bmatrix}
50 & 7.1 \\
100 & 7.2 \\
150 & 6.8 \\
200 & 7.2 \\
250 & 6.9 \\
300 & 6.9 \\
350 & 7.1 \\
400 & 6.9 \\
450 & 6.9 \\
500 & 6.8
\end{bmatrix}
$$

The previous use of two-digit precision is inappropriate for this type of convergence experiment. We change the precision to six digits and repeat the experiment. But first, a small aside for those who are wondering why their computer is showing exactly the same numbers as shown in this book. Where is the randomness? A pseudo random number generator has a definite start and a definite algorithm for determining the next output. Thus all computers will produce the same results as long as the same random experiments are carried out. To make the random number generator genuinely (pseudo-) random, we initialise the generator with a single simplification of the expression RANDOM(0).

❑   [O]ptions   [P]recision   Mode: [A]pproximate   Digits: 6   [↵]

   [A]uthor   random(0) =   [↵]

Simplify the above VECTOR expression once again.

$$
\#41: \begin{bmatrix}
50 & 7.14 \\
100 & 7.15 \\
150 & 6.88666 \\
200 & 6.935 \\
250 & 6.876 \\
300 & 7.03333 \\
350 & 6.71714 \\
400 & 6.995 \\
450 & 7.01333 \\
500 & 6.982
\end{bmatrix}
$$

It is apparent to the naked eye that the averages converge on the value 7. Similar experiments are possible for the variance VAR and the standard deviation STDEV, but slower convergences are observed.

Here are the definitions of the functions used in this example. The functions COUNT and RELFREQUENCY1 are helper functions:

#1: $COUNT(a, v) := DIMENSION(SELECT(v_i = a, i, 1, DIMENSION(v)))$

#2: $FREQUENCY(v) := VECTOR([k, COUNT(k, v)], k, 2, 12)$

#3: $RELFREQUENCY1(v, n) := VECTOR\left(\left[k, \dfrac{COUNT(k, v)}{n}\right], k, 2, 12\right)$

#4: $RELFREQUENCY(v) := RELFREQUENCY1(v, DIMENSION(v))$

#5: $likely := \left[\left[2, \dfrac{1}{36}\right], \left[3, \dfrac{2}{36}\right], \left[4, \dfrac{3}{36}\right], \left[5, \dfrac{4}{36}\right], \left[6, \dfrac{5}{36}\right], \left[7, \dfrac{6}{36}\right]\right.$

Example 3: From physics - a line of curvature

When a beam is curved by bending forces, there is a neutral axis, a line of zero stress inside the beam, that curves in reaction to the applied forces. The differential equation of this line $y(x)$ is $y'' = -\dfrac{M(x)}{E \cdot I}$, where E (the modulus of stretching or elasticity) and I (the moment of inertia) are taken as constants. For a beam under an evenly distributed load, resting on two supports, calculate the equation of $y(x)$, the place(s) and value(s) of maximal displacement and the points of inflection. The line should be visualised in an appropriate graphic.

Use $M(x) = \dfrac{q}{2}(ax - x^2)$ for the bending moment, where a is the distance between the two supports.

To prepare, let's define the unknown function $y(x)$ and the bending moment function $m(x)$.

❏ $\boxed{\text{A}}$uthor `y(x) :=` $\boxed{↵}$

$\boxed{\text{A}}$uthor `m(x) :=q/2 (ax-x^2)` $\boxed{↵}$

Now we can enter the differential equation $y'' = -\dfrac{M(x)}{E \cdot I}$:

❏ $\boxed{\text{A}}$uthor `dif(y(x),x,2)=-m(x)/(e i)` $\boxed{↵}$

```
#1:  Y(x) :=

                 q           2
#2:  M(x) :=  ───── ·(a·x − x )
                 2

        d  2           M(x)
#3:  [───]  Y(x) = − ────────
       dx              e·i
```

The stepwise solution of this equation starts with the first integration.

❏ $\boxed{\text{C}}$alculus $\boxed{\text{I}}$ntegrate ... answer all questions with $\boxed{↵}$
$\boxed{\text{S}}$implify $\boxed{↵}$

```
       ⌠   d  2           M(x)
#4:    | [[───]  Y(x) = − ──────] dx
       ⌡    dx             e·i

                       2
        d            q·x ·(2·x − 3·a)
#5:    ── Y(x) = ─────────────────────
        dx              12·e·i
```

In the same style as an integration table, DERIVE does not add an arbitrary constant. It is the responsibility of the user to add constants as needed. This is an ideal time to discuss this in a teaching situation. The addition of a constant is very simple, e.g. using the ⌷F3⌷ key.

❑   ⌷A⌷uthor ⌷F3⌷ +α ⌷↵⌷

$$\#6: \quad \frac{d}{dx} Y(x) = \frac{q \cdot x^2 \cdot (2 \cdot x - 3 \cdot a)}{12 \cdot e \cdot i} + \alpha$$

We integrate a second time and add the arbitrary constant β.

❑   ⌷C⌷alculus ⌷I⌷ntegrate ... answer all questions with ⌷↵⌷
     ⌷S⌷implify ⌷↵⌷
     ⌷A⌷uthor ⌷F3⌷ +β ⌷↵⌷

$$\#7: \quad \int \left[\frac{d}{dx} Y(x) = \frac{q \cdot x^2 \cdot (2 \cdot x - 3 \cdot a)}{12 \cdot e \cdot i} + \alpha \right] dx$$

$$\#8: \quad Y(x) = \frac{x \cdot (q \cdot x^3 - 2 \cdot a \cdot q \cdot x^2 + 24 \cdot \alpha \cdot e \cdot i)}{24 \cdot e \cdot i}$$

$$\#9: \quad Y(x) = \frac{x \cdot (q \cdot x^3 - 2 \cdot a \cdot q \cdot x^2 + 24 \cdot \alpha \cdot e \cdot i)}{24 \cdot e \cdot i} + \beta$$

Invoking the ›Expand‹ command changes the appearance of the solution somewhat:

❑   ⌷E⌷xpand ⌷↵⌷

$$\#10: Y(x) = \frac{x^4 \cdot q}{24 \cdot e \cdot i} - \frac{x^3 \cdot a \cdot q}{12 \cdot e \cdot i} + x \cdot \alpha + \beta$$

Expression #10 is the result of the stepwise solution of the above differential equation. Syntactically, expression #10 is an equation, with the (still) unknown function $y(x)$ on the left and the found solution of $y(x)$ on the right. In this form it is relatively simple to reformulate the equation as an assignment. We need only convert the $y(x) =$... into $y(x):=$... by adding a colon.

This is an ideal place to instruct students about the subtle but fundamental difference between an equation and an assignment or definition. This difference is rarely taught and is unknown to most students. The reason is that in mathematics we use the same symbol, the equals sign, for both because a mathematician knows the difference from context.

❑ $\boxed{\text{A}}$uthor $\boxed{\text{F3}}$

> AUTHOR expression: Y(x) = x^4·q/(24·e·i) − x^3·a·q/(12·e·i) + x·α + β_

Move the cursor in front of the equality sign.

> AUTHOR expression: Y(x)_= x^4·q/(24·e·i) − x^3·a·q/(12·e·i) + x·α + β

Insert the colon and finish with $\boxed{\leftarrow}$.

$$\#11: \quad Y(x) := \frac{x^4 \cdot q}{24 \cdot e \cdot i} - \frac{x^3 \cdot a \cdot q}{12 \cdot e \cdot i} + x \cdot \alpha + \beta$$

Now we must find two boundary conditions, so as to determine the values of the integration constants α and β. The conditions to be observed are:

- $y(0) = 0$, since the beam lies upon a support at the coordinate origin.
- $y(a) = 0$, since the beam lies upon a support at $x=a$.

The boundary conditions given above can be written directly as a system of equations and solved with the ›soLve‹ command for α and β.

❑ $\boxed{\text{A}}$uthor $[y(0)=0,y(a)=0]$ $\boxed{\leftarrow}$

so$\boxed{\text{L}}$ve $\boxed{\leftarrow}$ Variable: α $\boxed{\leftarrow}$ Variable: β $\boxed{\leftarrow}$

$$\#12: \quad [Y(0) = 0, \ Y(a) = 0]$$

$$\#13: \quad \left[\alpha = \frac{a^3 \cdot q}{24 \cdot e \cdot i}, \ \beta = 0 \right]$$

Once again we need to convert the equations into assignments.

❑ Copy expression #13 with $\boxed{\text{F3}}$ and insert colons.

$$\#14: \quad \left[\alpha := \frac{a^3 \cdot q}{24 \cdot e \cdot i}, \ \beta := 0 \right]$$

Now we can take a look at the final solution of the line.

❑   Ⓐuthor   y(x)   ⏎

    Ⓢimplify   ⏎

#15: Y(x)

$$\text{#16:} \quad \frac{q \cdot x^4}{24 \cdot e \cdot i} - \frac{a \cdot q \cdot x^3}{12 \cdot e \cdot i} + \frac{a^3 \cdot q \cdot x}{24 \cdot e \cdot i}$$

In order to find the point(s) of maximum displacement and the points of inflection, we have to move into a function discussion. We find the first derivative and name it *y1*.

❑   Ⓐuthor   dif(y(x),x)   ⏎

    Ⓢimplify   ⏎

    Ⓐuthor   y1(x) :=   F3   ⏎

$$\text{#17:} \quad \frac{d}{dx} \, Y(x)$$

$$\text{#18:} \quad \frac{q \cdot x^3}{6 \cdot e \cdot i} - \frac{a \cdot q \cdot x^2}{4 \cdot e \cdot i} + \frac{a^3 \cdot q}{24 \cdot e \cdot i}$$

$$\text{#19: Y1(x) :=} \quad \frac{q \cdot x^3}{6 \cdot e \cdot i} - \frac{a \cdot q \cdot x^2}{4 \cdot e \cdot i} + \frac{a^3 \cdot q}{24 \cdot e \cdot i}$$

Similarly we find the second derivative and name it *y2*.

❑   Ⓐuthor   dif(y1(x),x)   ⏎

    Ⓢimplify   ⏎

    Ⓐuthor   y2(x) :=   F3   ⏎

$$\text{#20:} \quad \frac{d}{dx} \, Y1(x)$$

$$\text{#21:} \quad \frac{q \cdot x^2}{2 \cdot e \cdot i} - \frac{a \cdot q \cdot x}{2 \cdot e \cdot i}$$

$$\text{#22: Y2(x) :=} \quad \frac{q \cdot x^2}{2 \cdot e \cdot i} - \frac{a \cdot q \cdot x}{2 \cdot e \cdot i}$$

The points of maximum displacement are the points at which the first derivative vanishes:

❑ $\boxed{A}$uthor y1(x) =0 $\boxed{↵}$

    so$\boxed{L}$ve $\boxed{↵}$ Variable: x $\boxed{↵}$

```
#23: Y1(x) = 0

              a
#24: x =  ───
              2

                ⎡ √3      1 ⎤
#25: x = a·⎢ ──  +  ── ⎥
                ⎣  2       2 ⎦

                ⎡ 1      √3 ⎤
#26: x = a·⎢ ──  -  ── ⎥
                ⎣ 2       2 ⎦
```

For the second and third solutions we can look at a numerical approximation.

❑ appro$\boxed{X}$ #25 $\boxed{↵}$

    appro$\boxed{X}$ #26 $\boxed{↵}$

```
#27: x = 1.36602·a

#28: x = - 0.366025·a
```

Since these both fall outside the bounds of possibility, i.e. the domain $0 \le x \le a$, they should be ignored. The remaining unique point of maximum displacement is $x = a/2$, the midpoint between the two supports. The value of the displacement can be simply calculated.

To determine the points of inflection, we find the points where the second derivative vanishes.

❑ $\boxed{A}$uthor y2(x) =0 $\boxed{↵}$

    so$\boxed{L}$ve $\boxed{↵}$ Variable: x $\boxed{↵}$

```
#29: Y2(x) = 0

#30: x = 0

#31: x = a
```

The two points of inflection are thus at the same point as the supports.

To present the line graphically, we need some values for the load q, the modulus of elasticity E, the moment of inertia I and the distance a between the supports, e.g.:

❑ $\boxed{\text{A}}$uthor [q:=24,e:=1,i:=-1,a:=1] $\boxed{\;↵\;}$

$\boxed{\text{A}}$uthor y(x) $\boxed{\;↵\;}$

$\boxed{\text{S}}$implify $\boxed{\;↵\;}$

$\boxed{\text{P}}$lot $\boxed{\text{B}}$eside $\boxed{\;↵\;}$ $\boxed{\text{P}}$lot

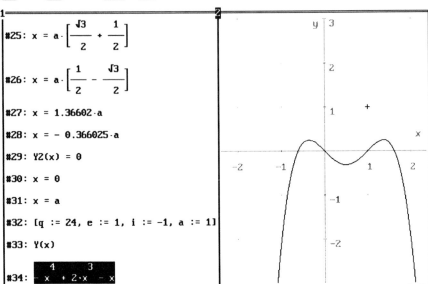

Since we are only interested in the region $0 \le x \le 1$, we vary the plot frame to suit:

❑ $\boxed{\text{R}}$ange ... select the borders as per the left picture $\boxed{\;↵\;}$

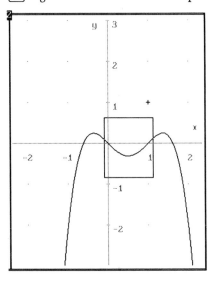

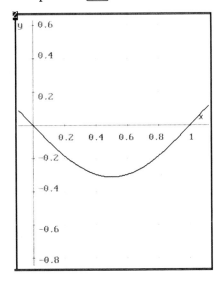

Example 4: Introduction to Taylor series

> With the help of some "favourite" function, develop a course unit that enables students to understand the Taylor series expansion.

We start with a motivation for dealing with this theme and present the following thoughts:

> "In a pocket calculator the four operations of addition, subtraction, multiplication and division are implemented. How can the calculator calculate the sine function with only these four operations? "

Furthermore there is the more general mathematical problem:

> "Can we approximate a function arbitrarily using only the four basic operations?"

With the assistance of the sine function we sketch an experimental introduction to the subject of Taylor polynomials. Many of the ideas used here originated with Bärbel Barzel in Düsseldorf.

❑ 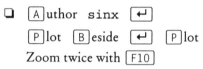 [A]uthor sinx [↵]

[P]lot [B]eside [↵] [P]lot

Zoom twice with [F10]

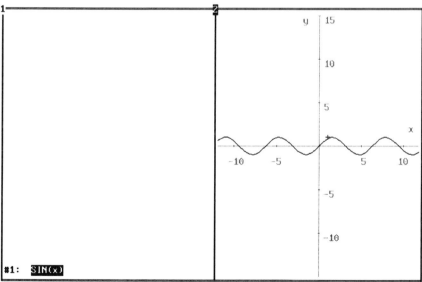

#1: SIN(x)

The students will use the built-in but still (to them) unknown function TAYLOR. The function can be directly entered or it can be reached via the ›Calculus Taylor‹

command. The students will apply TAYLOR to sin(*x*), simplify the result and plot it. (This approach is in the realm of our Scaffolding Method 6.)

❑   [C]alculus [T]aylor

The prompts for the expression and the variable are both to be replied to with [↵]. The prompts for the order of the polynomial and the expansion point, namely

| CALCULUS TAYLOR: Degree: **5** | Point: 0 |

are also to be replied to with [↵].

[S]implify [↵]

[P]lot [P]lot

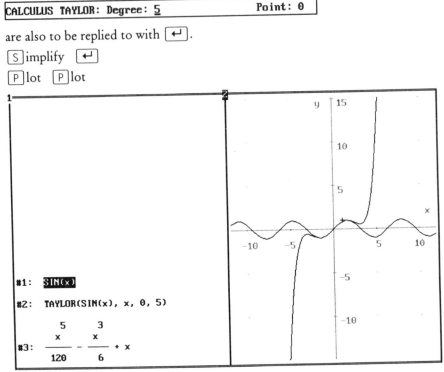

#1: SIN(x)

#2: TAYLOR(SIN(x), x, 0, 5)

$$\#3: \quad \frac{x^5}{120} - \frac{x^3}{6} + x$$

Expression #3 is presented as "the Taylor polynomial of order 5 corresponding to sin(*x*) around the point 0", whereby attention will also be directed to the arguments in expression #2. Then the students are asked to find the connection between the Taylor polynomials and the original function, where an answer like the following is expected:

> "The Taylor polynomial is, in the neighbourhood of the expansion point, a 'good' approximation of the original function."

Now the students are called upon to erase the last graph and expressions #2 and #3.

❑ [D]elete [L]ast

[A]lgebra [R]emove Start: 2 [⇤] Ende: 3 [↵]

Then the students should calculate and plot the Taylor polynomials of order 1 through 13 for the function sin(x).

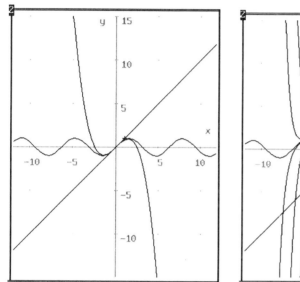
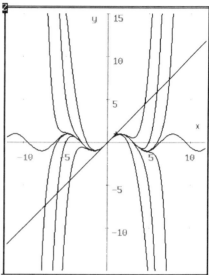

Now it is time for the students to examine the geometric connection between the Taylor polynomials and the original function, where we await the development of the following sort of understanding:

> "A higher order Taylor polynomial is closer to the original function and approximates it better. By better we mean that the domain in which the Taylor polynomial is a good approximation is larger."

An Aside: Experimentally realised understandings like those above are useful only for motivation and concept building, and should in no sense be seen as a replacement for a mathematically exact treatment. The empirical experiences and discoveries the students obtain during the experimental phase, such as the ideas of a "good approximation" or "better approximation" can be used as the starting point in a process of refining these formulations:

• When is a function a "good" approximation?

• When is one approximation "better" than another?

This relates to the educational goal of Description, brought up in Chapter 3.

Now back to the introduction to Taylor polynomials. What is behind the function TAYLOR, that, for the student, has been only a Black-Box until now? With the following question the students are encouraged to hone their powers of induction: "Can one predict how the Taylor polynomial of degree n around the point 0 for sin(x) will look?". In the process, they will be guided to collect the Taylor polynomials of order 1, 3, 5, 7 and 9 together, so as to see more clearly the similarities and differences. From the previous experiments most students will have already noted that the even orders do not bring anything new.

❏ $\boxed{\text{A}}$uthor vector([n,taylor(sinx,x,0,n)],n,1,9,2) $\boxed{\leftarrow}$

  $\boxed{\text{S}}$implify $\boxed{\leftarrow}$

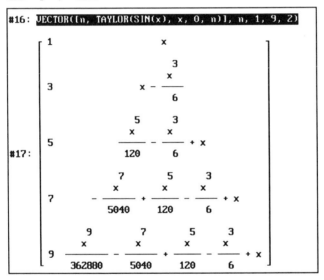

Practically every student recognises that the polynomials consist of only odd powers of x and that the signs of the coefficients alternate. Fewer students recognise that the denominators are all factorials, though this of course depends upon whether factorials have already been seen, and how they have been handled.

For further practice the same process can be carried out for $\cos(x)$ and for e^x.

After this the idea of a "good approximation" should be experimentally investigated. We describe two starting points: one based on calculation, the other a graphical method.

The calculation based approach evaluates the original function and the Taylor polynomial at various points, using two adjacent algebra windows so as to be able to lay the results next to one another.

❑ Close the graphics window should it be open.

Clear all expressions using ⊤ransfer ⊂lear Аll ↵

Аuthor sinx ↵

⊂alculus ⊤aylor ↵ Variable: x ↵ Degree: 5 ↵

Simplify ↵

Аuthor tp(x):= F3

Now we separate the window into two algebra windows.

❑ Window Split Vertical ↵

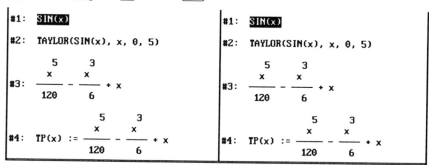

In the left window we evaluate the sine function and the Taylor polynomial at the point $x = 0.1$, in the right window we evaluate them at the point $x = 1.0$.

❑ Аuthor sin(0.1) ↵

appro X ↵

Аuthor tp(0.1) ↵

appro X ↵

Change to the right window and repeat the inputs for 1.0.

#5: SIN(0.1)	#5: SIN(1)
#6: 0.0998333	#6: 0.841470
#7: TP(0.1)	#7: TP(1)
#8: 0.0998334	#8: 0.841666

While the difference between the two values at $x = 0.1$ is only 0.0000001, it has grown considerably to 0.0001960 at $x = 1.0$, that is, it has grown by factor of almost two thousand.

The graphical approach for the selfsame investigation is to plot the two curves and then repeatedly zoom the plots around the areas of interest. Using the graphics cross, trace mode and other tools we can similarly find the actual numerical difference between the two curves.

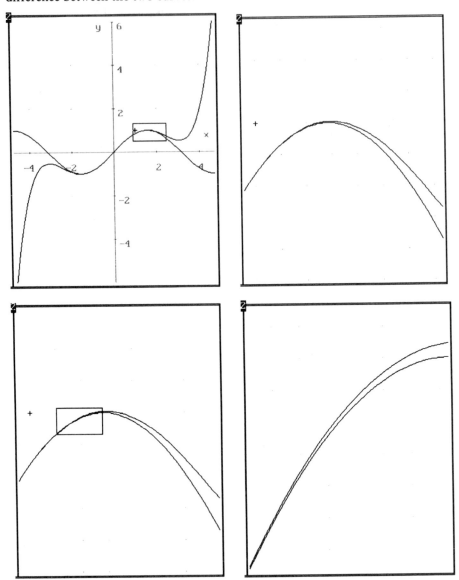

A further exercise that deepens the understanding of Taylor polynomials is the following: "Find a function that has a region in which the approximation is 'good' that does not increase no matter how high the order of the Taylor polynomial is".

The function $\dfrac{1}{1+x^2}$ around the point 0 has a convergence radius of 1, and is an example of such a function:

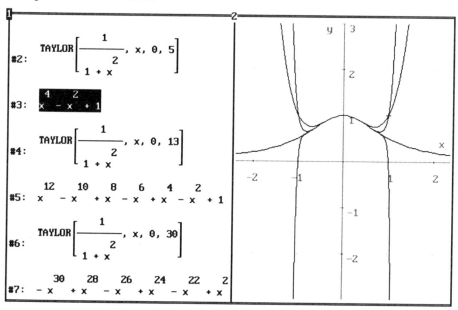

An alternative (or extended) introduction to the subject of Taylor polynomials starts with the problem:

> "Given a function and a point, find a polynomial of some given order such that the function value and the polynomial value at that point agree and the values of the first n derivatives of the polynomial and the function at that point agree."

Here only as many agreements of derivatives are possible as the number of unknowns in the polynomial, that is, one more than the degree of the polynomial. The author thanks David Sjöstrand of Sweden for this idea.

We stay with the sine function for now and look for a polynomial of degree 5 with the (unknown) coefficients a,b,c,d,e,f .

❑ 　Author `h(x):=sinx` ⏎

　　Author `p(x):=ax^5+bx^4+cx^3+dx^2+ex+f` ⏎

```
#1:  H(x) := SIN(x)

             5     4     3     2
#2:  P(x) := a·x + b·x + c·x + d·x + e·x + f
```

As our six requirements we demand that at the point $x = 0$ the function values and the first, second, third, fourth, and fifth derivatives agree. Since the function itself can be seen as the zero-th derivative, we obtain the following system of equations:

$$\left.\frac{d^n}{dx^n}h(x)\right|_{x=0} = \left.\frac{d^n}{dx^n}p(x)\right|_{x=0} \quad \text{for } n = 0,1,2,3,4,5$$

We use the equivalent formulation:

$$\left.\left(\frac{d^n}{dx^n}h(x) = \frac{d^n}{dx^n}p(x)\right)\right|_{x=0} \quad \text{for } n = 0,1,2,3,4,5$$

and solve this system in two steps. First we equate the derivatives, using the VECTOR function to collect all the equations in one expression. Then we substitute 0 for x in the resulting system of equations.

❑ 　Author `vector(dif(h(x),x,n)=dif(p(x),x,n),n,0,5)` ⏎

　　Simplify ⏎

```
#3:  VECTOR[[d/dx]^n H(x) = [d/dx]^n P(x), n, 0, 5]

        5     4     3     2                      4          3
#4:  [SIN(x) = a·x + b·x + c·x + d·x + e·x + f, COS(x) = 5·a·x + 4·b·x + 3
```

❑ 　Manage Substitute

```
MANAGE SUBSTITUTE value: x
```

Replace x with 0 ⏎

```
MANAGE SUBSTITUTE value: a
```

Ignore this and all other variables with ⏎

　　Simplify ⏎

```
               5       4      3      2                          4           3
#5:  [SIN(θ) = a·θ  + b·θ  + c·θ  + d·θ  + e·θ + f, COS(θ) = 5·a·θ  + 4·b·θ  + 3
#6:  [θ = f, 1 = e, 0 = 2·d, -1 = 6·c, θ = 24·b, 1 = 120·a]
```

The resulting system of equations is then solved.

❑ so⌊L⌋ve ⌊↵⌋

```
             1                1
#7:  [a = ─────, b = 0, c = - ───, d = 0, e = 1, f = 0]
            120               6
```

We calculate the Taylor polynomial with the ›Calculus Taylor‹ command and compare the two to check that both methods lead to the same result.

❑ ⌊A⌋uthor taylor(sinx,x,0,5) ⌊↵⌋

⌊S⌋implify ⌊↵⌋

```
#8:  TAYLOR(SIN(x), x, 0, 5)

         5     3
        x     x
#9:  ───── - ───── + x
       120     6
```

In the context of a comprehensive mathematical education, we can now speak about equivalent characterisations of an object. One of these characterisations is taken as the definition and the others must be proved to be equivalent to this definition. It must be made clear that the choice of which characterisation is the definition is completely arbitrary. It is to be noted though, that an appropriate selection can alleviate the amount of work required in proofs.

To close off we look back to the original question "How can a calculator calculate the sine function?". The student should now be able to give an answer to this question: it is possible to find a polynomial that between $-\pi/2$ and $\pi/2$ approximates the sine function "well enough". This polynomial is calculated once and programmed into the calculator. Then, using appropriate transformations such as $\sin(x) = \sin(x - 2\pi)$, $\sin(x) = \sin(\pi - x)$ to bring the argument $\sin(\alpha)$ within the interval $[-\pi/2, \pi/2]$, we can calculate $\sin(\alpha)$ for arbitrary values using the polynomial.

Example 5: Introduction to limits

Using the example of Carl Lewis and Alois Black from Chapter 3, develop a course that makes the idea of limits as clear as possible to students.

To reiterate quickly: Carl Lewis and Alois Black compete in a 100-metre dash. Carl runs 100m in 10 seconds while Alois needs 20. Carl gives Alois a handicap of 10 metres. Using the time-distance formula, we can show that Carl passes Alois 2 seconds after the start at the 20 metre mark.

Another way of approaching this situation results in a completely opposing result, that Carl will *never* pass Alois. Carl arrives at the point where Alois started after 1 second. In this second, Alois has run 5 metres. Carl needs a half second to reach this point. But in this half second, Alois has run 2.5 metres further. Carrying this on, Alois is always ahead of Carl.

Our experience agrees with the time-distance formula. What is wrong with the second formulation?

The student should perform the investigation independently, experimenting with the computer as much as he wants. The average student will need tips from the teacher as to which directions to try. In the following we look at one possible method.

Tip 1: Draw up (by hand) a table that explains who is where and when. The following information should appear in each row of the table: (a) observation number, (b) elapsed time since the last observation, (c) total elapsed time, (d) how many metres Carl has run and (e) how many metres Alois has run.

A student's table could appear as follows:

observation number	elapsed time since the last observation	total elapsed time	metres Carl has run	metres Alois has run
1. observ.	0 sec	0 sec	0 m	10 m
2. observ.	1 sec	1 sec	10 m	15 m
3. observ.	$\frac{1}{2}$ sec	$1+\frac{1}{2} = 1.5$ sec	15 m	17.5 m
4. observ.	$\frac{1}{4}$ sec	$1+\frac{1}{2}+\frac{1}{4} = 1.75$ sec	17.5 m	18.75 m
5. observ.	$\frac{1}{8}$ sec	$1+\frac{1}{2}+\frac{1}{4}+\frac{1}{8} = 1.875$ sec	18.75 m	19.375 m

The length to which the student should extend this table has two deciding factors. First, the student needs a certain minimal level of manual work to get a feel of the inductive structure (see the corresponding educational goal in Chapter 3). Second, the computer should only be used where it will bring some benefit, where its use can be justified. In any case, the table above does not have enough detail to show clear and convincing tendencies. These appear only after 10, 20, 30 observations. Continuing the table so far by hand is not at all reasonable. It would be better to apply the computer to the problem.

The teacher should prepare the functions used in the following and give them to the students as experimental tools (see Scaffolding Method 2). We provide the function definitions at the end of this section. We should shift to approximate calculations with 22-digit precision in preparation.

❑ [O]ptions [P]recision Mode: [A]pproximate Digits: 22 [↵]

Tip 2: Load the file EXAMPLE5.MTH (see the end of this chapter for the contents of this file). When you simplify the expression CARL_ALOIS(m), then the table above (except the second row) will be calculated, down to the *m*-th row. From this table eleven representative rows will be shown; eleven rows fit exactly on the screen. Experiment with this function and formulate some hypotheses about the problem.

❑ [T]ransfer [L]oad [U]tility example5 [↵]

    [A]uthor carl_alois(10) [↵]

    [S]implify [↵]

	observ	time_total	metre_carl	metre_alois
	1	0	0	10
	2	1	10	15
	3	1.5	15	17.5
	4	1.75	17.5	18.75
#4:	5	1.875	18.75	19.375
	6	1.9375	19.375	19.6875
	7	1.96875	19.6875	19.84375
	8	1.984375	19.84375	19.921875
	9	1.9921875	19.921875	19.9609375
	10	1.99609375	19.9609375	19.98046875
	11	1.998046875	19.98046875	19.990234375

Let's see if the trend appearing here becomes amplified when we take 20 instead of 10 observations.

❑   Ａuthor `carl_alois(20)` ↵

Ｓimplify ↵

#5: CARL_ALOIS(20)

observ	time_total	metre_carl	metre_alois
1	0	0	10
3	1.5	15	17.5
5	1.875	18.75	19.375
7	1.96875	19.6875	19.84375
9	1.9921875	19.921875	19.9609375
11	1.998046875	19.98046875	19.990234375
13	1.99951171875	19.9951171875	19.99755859375
15	1.9998779296875	19.998779296875	19.9993896484375
17	1.999969482421875	19.99969482421875	19.99984741210937
19	1.99999237060546875	19.9999237060546875	19.999961853027343
21	1.9999980926513671875	19.999980926513671875	19.9999904632568359

#6:

That should be convincing! The second column shows us that regardless of how often we make our observations, we never get past the two-second mark, in fact, we never even *get* to the two-second mark. That means: regardless of how often (even infinitely often) we make observations, every one of them deals with the time *before* Carl passes Alois. Similarly the third and fourth columns show that the 20-metre mark is the point at which this overtaking takes place. If this numerical material is not enough to convince the sceptics, they can carry on further, with CARL_ALOIS(30) or even CARL_ALOIS(40).

Now we hope that the student connects the observations above with the previously seen time-distance formula from Chapter 3. Thus we go on to the following:

Tip 3: Remember the calculation of the overtaking time and place using the time-distance formula for Carl ($D\_CARL(t) = 10 \cdot t$) and for Alois ($D\_ALOIS(t) = 10 + 5 \cdot t$) made at the beginning of this section. We want to find out what these formulae and the above tables have in common. With the CARL function you can obtain the two columns in the table above that give Carl's time and distance and thus give the values for the time and distance diagram. Similarly for the function ALOIS. Experiment with both functions numerically and graphically.

❏   [A]uthor   `carl(10)`   [↵]

    [S]implify   [↵]

    [P]lot   [B]eside   [↵]

    [P]lot   (left picture)

Since only one point is visible, the dimensions of the axes must be altered to see all the points.

❏   [S]cale   x: 2   [⇆]   y: 10   [↵]   (right picture)

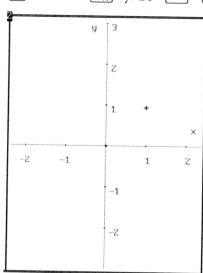
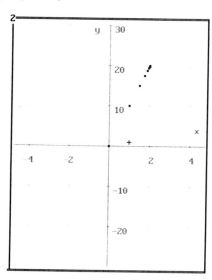

❏   [A]uthor   `alois(10)`   [↵]

    [S]implify   [↵]

    [P]lot   [P]lot

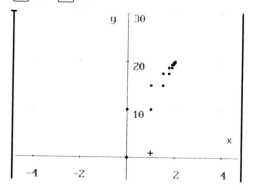

Tip 4: Investigate the immediate neighbourhood of the point (2,20) using the possibilities provided by the graphics window (graphics cross, arbitrary plot framing, etc.).

❑ [M]ove x: 2 [⇥] y: 20 [↵]

   [R]ange ... select frame as per the left picture [↵]

   [R]ange ... select frame as per the centre picture [↵]

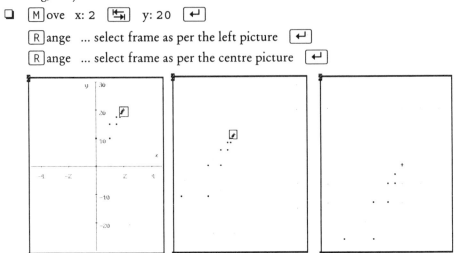

One sees here what was also apparent from the numerical table: the observations approach the point (2,20) from below left, without ever actually reaching the point.

Tip 5: Calculate and plot CARL(20) and ALOIS(20). The gaps between the previously plotted points and the point (2,20) are filled. Repeat the zooming above, until a similar picture to the one on the right appears.

This game can be arbitrarily prolonged until calculation inaccuracies appear when the axis scale becomes of the same order as the graphics window calculating accuracy. To prevent this, raise the calculation accuracy of the graphics window.

To finish off we add the straight line plots for the time and distance formulae for Carl and Alois to the discrete time observation plots. We then recognise that the points are just special cases of the lines.

❑ [A]uthor d_carl(t):=10t [↵]

   [P]lot [P]lot

   [A]uthor d_alois(t):=10+5t [↵]

   [P]lot [P]lot

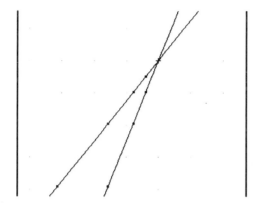

The students must now give an answer to the question posed at the beginning of the section. The following is a possible formulation. This example meets three of the educational goals presented in Chapter 3: Relativity of Representations (see in particular the example of the so-called Drudel), Description and Argumentation.

> "The seeming paradox has its origins in the fact that the second collection of pointwise observations looks at only one part of the race. That is, we observe only the first two seconds of the race, the time after this not being observed at all. Performing arbitrarily many observations covers over this significant and deceptive restriction."

A fundamental and deep realisation, of which this result provides a good example, is:

> "Things can be infinite but bounded."

The example suggested by the false answer is the division of the finite period of two seconds into an infinite number of pieces, namely:

$$2 = 0 + 1 + 1/2 + 1/4 + 1/8 + 1/16 + ...$$

We go on now with a description of how this and other infinite sums can be investigated.

The previously prepared function TIME gives the time that has passed since the start: TIME(n) is the time that passes up to the n-th observation: TIME(1)=0, TIME(2)=1, TIME(3)=1+1/2 =1.5, TIME(4)=1+1/2+1/4 =1.75, etc. TIME(n) is the sum of the first n numbers in the infinite sequence described above.

Tip 6: Calculate TIME(n) for the values $n = 1,2,3,10,15,20,30$. What value do the results tend towards? Apply the limit command to TIME(n), by entering:

❑   [A]uthor time(n)   [↵]

[C]alculus [L]imit   [↵]

CALCULUS LIMIT variable: n

Accept the variable with [↵] .

CALCULUS LIMIT: Point: 0   From:(Both)Left Right

Accept the point and the direction with [↵] .

lim TIME(n) #18: n→∞

The resulting expression #18 is to be read as "the limit of TIME(n) as n approaches infinity". It describes the number towards which the value of TIME(n) tends, as n grows larger, i.e. as n tends toward infinity. The ›Simplify‹ command calculates the value.

❑   [S]implify   [↵]

#19: 2

The calculated limit agrees with the supposed limit: 2 is the limit of the sequence TIME(1), TIME(2), TIME(3), TIME(4), etc. One can also imagine the limit as the *infinity-th* element of the sequence.

The function SEQUENCEPOINTS(t(n), n, m) calculates the first m points for a graphical representation of the sequence $t(n)$, where the points have the form $(i / t(i))$. In the following we calculate the first ten points of the sequence TIME(n), plot the result and find an appropriate axis scale. Before we go on to calculate the first 20 elements of the sequence, we change to 22 digit precision.

❑   [A]uthor sequencepoints(time(n),n,10)   [↵]

Simplify and plot the expression.

[S]cale x: 10 [⇥] y: 1 [↵]

[O]ptions [P]recision [⇥] Digits: 22 [↵]

[A]uthor sequencepoints(time(n),n,20)   [↵]

Simplify and plot the expression.

Plot the previously calculated limit (i.e. the number 2).

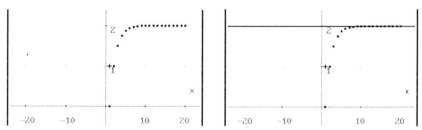

From the ninth point on, the points seem to lie upon the line. Due to our numerical experiments, we know that this is a (visual) trick. To see this graphically, we target one of the points apparently lying on the line:

❏ Move the graphics cross to the coordinates (15,2).

[C]enter   (in order to make the frames appear as in the left picture)

Zoom, until the axis scale is displayed 'x : 10^-3 y : 10^-4'.

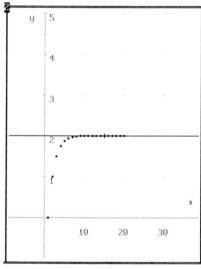
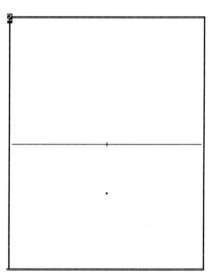

With enough zooming it becomes clear that the point does not reach the limit represented by the line. If one moves to the twentieth point, i.e. to the coordinates (20,2), the point seems to lie upon the line (with the current magnification).

❏ [M]ove x: 20 [⇥] y: 2 [↵]

[C]enter

Further zooming will show that this point lies under the line. This game can be continued indefinitely, until even the most sceptical student is convinced. One must only be careful that, at very high magnification, the calculation precision is high enough to limit the effects of rounding errors.

The infinitely distant limits are experimentally unreachable, because it is not possible to calculate an infinite number of sequence elements, or to press the zoom key an infinite number of times. Mathematical methods, and this is the wonder, allow us to manipulate this limit value and thus, so to speak, make a step into the infinite. In DERIVE these mathematical methods are available as the ›Calculus Limit‹ command and the LIM function.

The following are the definitions of the functions used in the examples in this section:

- TIME(n) returns the elapsed time up to the n-th observation..

    ```
    zeit(n):=sum(1/2^j,j,0,n-2)
    ```

- TAB(m) calculates a table with four columns: (a) the observation number, (b) the elapsed time, (c) the distance already run by Carl and (d) the distance already run by Alois. From the observations obtained in this way an appropriate sample of 11 is displayed.

    ```
    tab(m):=vector([j,time(j),10time(j),10+5time(j)],
        j,1,10floor(m/10)+1,floor(m/10))
    ```

- CARL_ALOIS(m) prepends the table calculated by TAB(m) with a title.

    ```
    carl_alois(m):=append(
    [[observ,time_total,metre_carl,metre_alois]],tab(m))
    ```

- CARL(m) calculates a table of Carl's performance up to the m-th observation. 11 rows are displayed.

    ```
    carl(m):=vector([time(i),10time(i)],
        i,1,10floor(m/10)+1,floor(10/m))
    ```

- ALOIS(m) calculates a table of Alois' performance up to the m-th observation. 11 rows are displayed.

    ```
    alois(m):=vector([time(i),10+5time(i)],
        i,1,10floor(m/10)+1,floor(10/m))
    ```

- SEQUENCEPOINTS(t,n,m) calculates the first m points in the sequence $t(n)$.

    ```
    sequencepoints(t,n,m):=vector([i,lim(t,n,i)],i,1,m)
    ```

Example 6: Introduction to integration

Using the origins of the Riemann sum, develop a course to introduce students to integration, the goal being the calculation of the surface areas of regions with curvilinear borders.

In the sense of Method 5 of the Scaffolding we help the students define functions for the following calculation methods. Each should be a generalisation of the previous:

- Sums of upper and lower rectangles for x^2 between 0 and 2
- Sums of upper and lower rectangles for x^2 between a and b
- Sums of upper and lower rectangles for $f(x)$ between a and b
- Trapezoid sum for $f(x)$ between a and b

We assume that the students know the surface area formulae for rectangles and trapezoids.

To start the course on Integration we give the following as motivation:

"We need the surface area between the graph $f(x):=x^2$ and the x-axis over the range $0 \le x \le 2$."

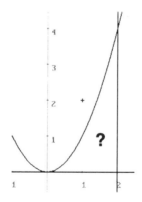

In discussion with the students we develop the idea that the area could be approximated by the sum of appropriately chosen rectangles. With this in mind, we limit ourselves to surfaces where only one edge is curvilinear, and the other (straight) edges all are at right angles to one another:

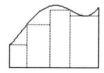

There are an infinite number of ways to approximate the surface as a sum of
rectangles. A simplifying restriction is to limit ourselves to rectangles of equal
width. When we further require that every rectangle lies completely inside the area,
there is only the possibility shown in the left hand diagram below (for 6 rectangles).
The sum of the areas of such a collection of rectangles is a lower bound for the area
of the surface, and is called a *lower sum*.

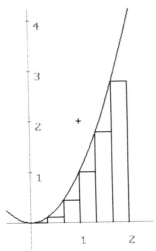
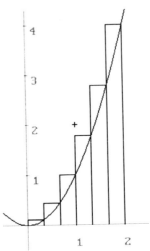

If we require the converse, that the surface lies completely inside the rectangles, we
obtain the right hand picture (for 6 rectangles). The sum of the areas of these
rectangles is an upper bound for the desired surface area and is called an *upper sum*.

Then we develop the idea that the approximation using upper and lower sums will
be better when the rectangles are smaller, i.e. the more rectangles we have. To
experiment with this idea, we define some functions in the following with which
one can plot the rectangles and calculate the resulting surface area.

Before we can plot a sequence of rectangles, we need to be able to plot a single
rectangle. Observing our special case (one edge lies on the x-axis in all cases), we
need only three arguments, the coordinates a and b and the height h. The rectangle
is then defined by the four corner points, as in the following definition.

❑ Ⓐuthor `rectangle(a,b,h):=[[a,0],[a,h],[b,h],[b,0]]` ⏎

    Ⓐuthor `rectangle(1,2,3/2)` ⏎

    Plot the last expression.

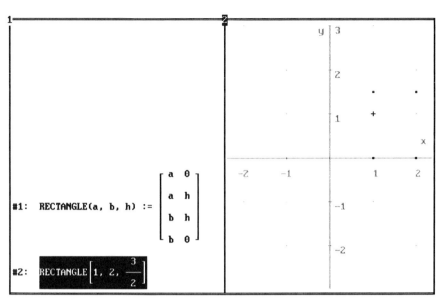

$$\text{#1:} \quad \text{RECTANGLE}(a, b, h) := \begin{bmatrix} a & 0 \\ a & h \\ b & h \\ b & 0 \end{bmatrix}$$

$$\text{#2:} \quad \text{RECTANGLE}\left[1, 2, \frac{3}{2}\right]$$

In order to plot the rectangle with sides and small corner points, the following graphics window settings must be changed.

❑ [O]ptions [S]tate [⇆] Mode: [C]onnected Size: [S]mall [↵]

  [D]elete [A]ll (in order to clear the large plotted corner points)

  [P]lot (in order to plot the rectangle again)

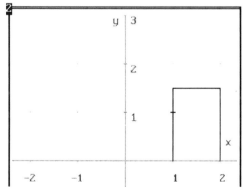

The following problems are to be solved for the function x^2 over the range $0 \le x \le 2$. Thus we prepare a plot of this function with the appropriate axes. That is, we choose the axes to put the interval $0 \le x \le 2$ in the centre of the plot.

❑ [D]elete [A]ll

  [A]lgebra [A]uthor x^2 [↵]

⎡P⎤lot ⎡P⎤lot

⎡M⎤ove x: 1 ⎣↹⎦ y: 2 ⎣↵⎦   (this point should become the centre)

⎡C⎤enter

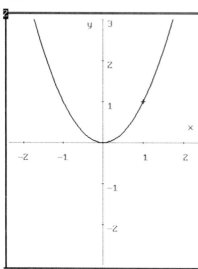
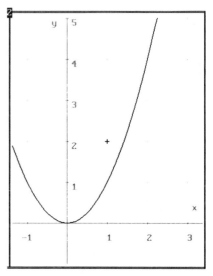

The following functions are to be derived by all the students with guidance from the teacher. The first function called L_RECTANGLE takes a single argument n (= the number of subdivisions of the interval) and returns a vector with the n lower sum rectangles. It should be created with reference to the RECTANGLE function. For this function the built-in function VECTOR is to be used to perform the chopping up of the interval $0 \leq x \leq 2$ into n equal pieces, namely

$$0, \frac{2}{n}, \frac{4}{n}, \frac{6}{n}, ..., \frac{2i}{n}, ..., \frac{2(n-2)}{n}, \frac{2(n-1)}{n}, 2$$

The completed function is tested with $n = 6, 10, 16$.

❑ ⎡A⎤uthor   l_rectangle(n) :=

   vector(rectangle(i 2/n, (i+1)2/n, (i 2/n)^2), i, 0, n-1) ⎣↵⎦

   Approximate and plot the expression l_rectangle(6).

   Clear everything and plot x^2 fresh.

   Approximate and plot the expression l_rectangle(10).

   Repeat the above for l_rectangle(16).

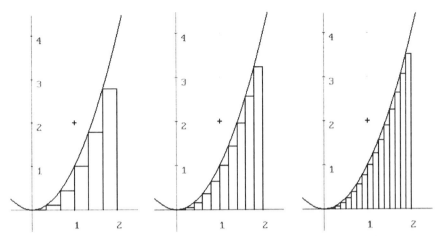

Now we define a function to calculate the lower sums, i.e. the sum of the areas of the lower rectangles. This function should be called L_SUM. First we calculate the area of the *i*-th lower sum rectangle as the product of its width (= width of the interval, $2/n$) and its height (= function value at the left interval end, $(i \cdot 2/n)^2$).

❑ [A]uthor   (2/n) (2i/n)^2 [↵]

Then we need to sum over all the rectangles. This is most easily performed using the sum operator.

❑ [C]alculus [S]um [↵] [↵]

| CALCULUS SUM: Lower limit: **1**   Upper limit: n |

Change the lower limit to 0, the upper limit to $n-1$.

[A]uthor l_sum(n) := [F3]   [↵]

$$\#13:\ \text{L\_SUM(n)} := \sum_{i=0}^{n-1} \frac{2}{n} \cdot \left[\frac{2 \cdot i}{n}\right]^2$$

We calculate the lower sum for $n = 6, 10, 100, 1000$.

❑ [A]uthor l_sum(6) [↵]

appro[X] [↵]

Repeat this for l_sum(10), l_sum(100), l_sum(1000).

| #14: L_SUM(6) |
| #15: 2.03703 |
| #16: L_SUM(10) |
| #17: 2.28 |

```
#18:  L_SUM(100)

#19:  2.62679

#20:  L_SUM(1000)

#21:  2.66266
```

The students should then *independently* define and test the functions U_RECTANGLE for the upper sum rectangles and U_SUM for the upper sum, i.e. the sum of the areas of the upper sum rectangles.

❏ [A]uthor   u_rectangle(n) :=

   vector(rectangle(2i/n,(i+1)2/n,((i+1)2/n)^2),i,0,n-1) [↵]

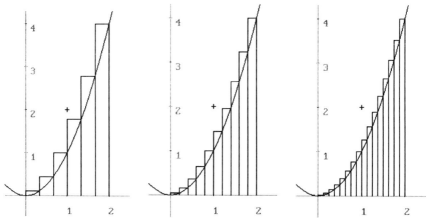

❏ [A]uthor   (2/n)(2(i+1)/n)^2 [↵]

   [C]alculus [S]um [↵] [↵]

Change the lower limit to 0, the upper limit to $n-1$.

[A]uthor u_sum(n) := [F3]   [↵]

$$\#31:\ U\_SUM(n) := \sum_{i=0}^{n-1} \frac{2}{n} \cdot \left[\frac{2 \cdot (i+1)}{n}\right]^2$$

Since the lower sum gives a lower bound for the actual surface area F and the upper sum gives an upper bound leads us to be able to state for all n:

$$F \in [\text{L\_SUM}(n), \text{U\_SUM}(n)]$$

Thus one can obtain a good approximation for F, in that one looks at such intervals for large values of n.

❏ [A]uthor   [l_sum(10000),u_sum(10000)] [↵]

appro⊠ ⏎
Ⓐuthor   [l_sum(100000),u_sum(100000)] ⏎
appro⊠ ⏎

```
#32: [L_SUM(10000), U_SUM(10000)]

#33: [2.66626, 2.66706]

#34: [L_SUM(100000), U_SUM(100000)]

#35: [2.66662, 2.66670]
```

From these observations one would estimate that F has the value $2.666... = 2.\dot{6} = 8/3$. To check (and confirm) this we calculate the limits of L_SUM(n) and U_SUM(n) for n tending to infinity.

❑ Ⓐuthor   [l_sum(n),u_sum(n)] ⏎

   Ⓒalculus Ⓛimit ⏎ variable: n ⏎ Point: inf ⏎

   Ⓢimplify ⏎

```
#36: [L_SUM(n), U_SUM(n)]

         lim  [L_SUM(n), U_SUM(n)]
#37: n→∞

        ⎡ 8    8 ⎤
#38: ⎢ —— , —— ⎥
        ⎣ 3    3 ⎦
```

Now the integral $\int_0^2 x^2 dx$ can be introduced as this value. We show how simple integration calculus is with a computer and use the same example to demonstrate.

❑ Ⓐuthor   x^2 ⏎

   Ⓒalculus Ⓘntegrate ⏎ variable: x ⏎

        Lower limit: 0 ⇥ Upper limit: 2 ⏎

   Ⓢimplify ⏎

```
           2
#39: x

           2
        ⌠    2
#40: ⎮  x   dx
        ⌡
        0

         8
#41: ——
         3
```

In a second stage we make a generalisation of the previous problem, in that we wish
to calculate the surface area between the graph of x^2 and the x-axis between the
bounds a and b. Thus the functions we already have for rectangles and the upper
and lower sums need to be modified to allow us to give the limits of integration as
arguments. To prepare we generalise the subdivision of the interval $[0,2]$,

$$0, \frac{2}{n}, \frac{4}{n}, \frac{6}{n}, ..., \frac{2i}{n}, ..., \frac{2(n-2)}{n}, \frac{2(n-1)}{n}, 2$$

to a subdivision of the interval $[a,b]$ into n pieces:

$$a, a+\frac{b-a}{n}, a+2\frac{b-a}{n}, ..., a+i\frac{b-a}{n}, ...a+(n-1)\frac{b-a}{n}, b$$

Then the students should modify the functions L_RECTANGLE, U_RECTANGLE,
L_SUM and U_SUM. Sample correct solutions are:

❑ [A]uthor l_rectangle(a,b,n):=
    vector(rectangle(a+i(b-a)/n,a+(i+1)(b-a)/n,
          (a+i(b-a)/n)^2),i,0,n-1) [↵]

[A]uthor u_rectangle(a,b,n):=
    vector(rectangle(a+i(b-a)/n,a+(i+1)(b-a)/n,
          (a+(i+1)(b-a)/n)^2),i,0,n-1) [↵]

[A]uthor l_sum(a,b,n):=
        sum((b-a)/n (a+i(b-a)/n)^2,i,0,n-1) [↵]

[A]uthor u_sum(a,b,n):=
        sum((b-a)/n (a+(i+1)(b-a)/n)^2,i,0,n-1) [↵]

In a test the new functions must give the same answers for $a = 0$ and $b = 2$ as the
old functions. The test for $n = 6$ confirms this and gives us a (strong) indication
for the correctness of the function definition.

❑ [A]uthor   l_sum(0,2,6) [↵]
appro[X] [↵]
[A]uthor   u_sum(0,2,6) [↵]   appro[X] [↵]

```
#46: L_SUM(0, 2, 100)

#47: 2.62679

#48: U_SUM(0, 2, 100)

#49: 2.70679
```

The functions derived in this way can be used in many ways upon the function x^2, for example:

- For approximate calculation of actual surface areas, e.g. for $a = 2$ and $b = 5$ with $n = 25$ respectively $n = 500$:

```
#50: [L_SUM(2, 5, 25), U_SUM(2, 5, 25)]

#51: [37.7472, 40.2672]

#52: [L_SUM(2, 5, 500), U_SUM(2, 5, 500)]

#53: [38.9370, 39.0630]
```

- Together with the limit command, to calculate exact values of actual surface areas, e.g. for $a = 2$ and $b = 5$:

```
#54: [L_SUM(2, 5, n), U_SUM(2, 5, n)]

     lim [L_SUM(2, 5, n), U_SUM(2, 5, n)]
#55: n→∞

#56: [39, 39]
```

- To calculate approximations of the surface area between two undetermined bounds a and b, e.g. for $n = 10$:

```
#57: [L_SUM(a, b, 10), U_SUM(a, b, 10)]
```

$$
\#58: \left[\frac{(b - a) \cdot (77 \cdot a^2 + 66 \cdot a \cdot b + 57 \cdot b^2)}{200}, \frac{(b - a) \cdot (57 \cdot a^2 + 66 \cdot a \cdot b + 77 \cdot b^2)}{200} \right]
$$

- Together with the limit command to calculate exact formulae for the surface area between two indefinite bounds a and b. The following three adjacent windows show the limit of the lower sums, the limit of the upper sums and the integral calculated using the command ›Calculus Integrate‹. The results from the limit function are expanded with the ›Expand‹ command to show them in their commonly known form.

$$
\#59: \lim_{n\to\infty} L\_SUM(a, b, n)
$$

$$
\#60: \frac{(a^2 + a \cdot b + b^2) \cdot (b - a)}{3}
$$

$$
\#61: \frac{b^3}{3} - \frac{a^3}{3}
$$

$$
\#62: \lim_{n\to\infty} U\_SUM(a, b, n)
$$

$$
\#63: \frac{(a^2 + a \cdot b + b^2) \cdot (b - a)}{3}
$$

$$
\#64: \frac{b^3}{3} - \frac{a^3}{3}
$$

$$
\#65: x^2
$$

$$
\#66: \int_a^b x^2 \, dx
$$

$$
\#67: \frac{b^3}{3} - \frac{a^3}{3}
$$

As a third stage the functions of the previous stage should be further generalised to calculate the surface area bounded by an arbitrary graph $f(x)$ and the x-axis between the bounds a and b. Thus we need to modify the previous functions again to allow the passing of the function as an argument.

In each place where a square was calculated (the previous function was, after all, x^2), we now need to calculate the function value. We need to take the function f and evaluate it at a point a. Since the function is given as a function term, i.e. as $f(x)$, defined as, e.g. $\sin(x) + x$, we require a programmed substitution of the form:

$$apply(f(x),x,a) := f(x)\big|_{x=a} \quad \text{respectively} \quad apply(t,x,a) := t\big|_{x=a}$$

The limit function LIM does exactly this, so to use a more understandable name like APPLY, we make a definition to rename the function.

❏ ⎡A⎤uthor   `apply(t,x,a):=lim(t,x,a)`   ⎡↵⎤

APPLY can be demonstrated with the following examples.

```
         APPLY(t, x, a)  := lim t
#68:                        x→a

                 2
#69: APPLY((x + 1) , x, 2) = 9

#70: APPLY(3·(x - y), x, b + 1) = - 3·(y - b - 1)
```

The students then need to redefine the functions L_RECTANGLE, U_RECTANGLE, L_SUM and U_SUM, so that the function term and the function variable are passed as arguments. The previously performed calculations with the function x^2 give many test examples for the new functions.

Here is a sample correct solution, with the differences to the last solutions printed in bold for clarity.

❏ ⎡A⎤uthor `l_rectangle(`**`t,x,`**`a,b,n):=`
     `vector(rectangle(a+i(b-a)/n,a+(i+1)(b-a)/n,`
         `apply(t,x,``a+i(b-a)/n)),i,0,n-1)`   ⎡↵⎤

⎡A⎤uthor `u_rectangle(`**`t,x,`**`a,b,n):=`
     `vector(rectangle(a+i(b-a)/n,a+(i+1)(b-a)/n,`
         `apply(t,x,``a+(i+1)(b-a)/n)),i,0,n-1)`   ⎡↵⎤

⎡A⎤uthor `l_sum(`**`t,x,`**`a,b,n):=`
     `sum((b-a)/n `**`apply(t,x,`**`a+i(b-a)/n),i,0,n-1)`   ⎡↵⎤

⎡A⎤uthor `u_sum(`**`t,x,`**`a,b,n):=`
     `sum((b-a)/n `**`apply(t,x,`**`a+(i+1)(b-a)/n),i,0,n-1)`   ⎡↵⎤

An application of these functions upon $\sqrt{x+2}$ gives the following:

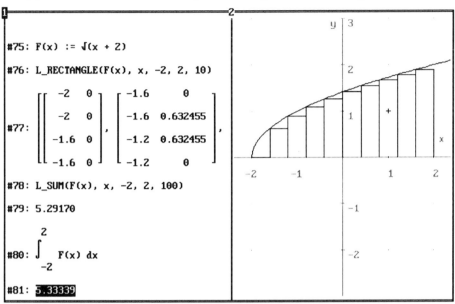

The attempt to obtain the correct answer 16/3, that can be directly calculated by simplifying the definite integral (expression #80) using the limit command, fails.

❏ ⟨S⟩implify #80 ⟨↵⟩

⟨A⟩uthor `lim(l_sum(f(x),x,-2,2,n),n,inf)` ⟨↵⟩

⟨S⟩implify ⟨↵⟩

```
        16
#82:  ─────
        3

        lim  L_SUM(F(x), x, -2, 2, n)
#83:  n→∞

                3/2 FLOOR(1/n) - 1
#84:  8·lim  n    ·     Σ          √i
        n→0+              i=0
```

Thus we see a bound of either the power of the limit function or of our methods of calculating surface areas via sums of rectangles. If it is the fundamental impossibility of calculating this limit or due to the implementation, we do not know.

Next we look at the surface area of the cosine function between $-\pi/2$ and $\pi/2$. For this we use the functions L_RECTANGLE and U_RECCTANGLE.

❏ ⟨A⟩uthor `l_rectangle(cosx,x,-pi/2,pi/2,10)` ⟨↵⟩

appro⌈X⌋ ⌈↵⌋

Plot the rectangles (left hand picture).

⌈A⌋uthor `u_rectangle(cosx,x,-pi/2,pi/2,10)` ⌈↵⌋

appro⌈X⌋ ⌈↵⌋

Clear the old ones and plot the new rectangles (right hand picture).

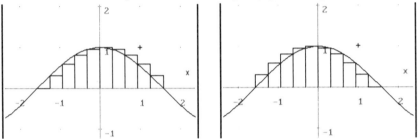

Obviously these are neither upper or lower sum rectangles, and the students are then instructed to find the problem. We aim for a recognition similar to:

> "The method used in the above definitions, that the function value at the left respectively right hand bound of the rectangle is taken to be the height of the rectangle, only works for monotonously increasing functions. Thus, for more general cases, a more complicated method of determining the rectangle height will be necessary."

It would thus be "more honest" to rename the functions defined above L_RECTANGLE, R_RECTANGLE, L_SUM and R_SUM.

It has been intended that the students experience the trials and tribulations of the method of upper and lower sums, as well as its limitations. These difficulties and limitations have historically led to a very elegant integral calculus. The way we have gone about this follows the genetic principle mentioned in Chapter 3.

Trapezoids are a very useful alternative to rectangles. As shown in the following picture, many surfaces can be closely approximated with few trapezoids (in the picture there are four trapezoids for $\cos(x)$ between $-\pi/2$ and $\pi/2$).

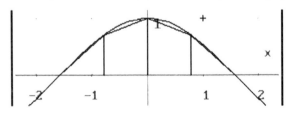

On the basis of their experience with rectangles, the students should independently define and test functions TRAPEZOID and TRAPEZOID_SUM. A sample solution follows.

❑ [A]uthor

$$\mathrm{trapezoid}(a,\alpha,b,\beta):=[[a,0],[a,\alpha],[b,\beta],[b,0]]\quad \boxed{\hookleftarrow}$$

[A]uthor `trapezoids(t,x,a,b,n):=`

`vector(trapezoid(a+i(b-a)/n,apply(t,x,a+i(b-a)/n),`

`a+(i+1)(b-a)/n,apply(t,x,a+(i+1)(b-a)/n)),i,0,n-1)` $\boxed{\hookleftarrow}$

[S]chreibe `trapezoid_sum(t,x,a,b,n):=`

`sum((apply(t,x,a+i(b-a)/n)+apply(t,x,a+(i+1)(b-a)/n))`

$$(b-a)/(2n),i,0,n-1)\quad \boxed{\hookleftarrow}$$

The students should compare the rectangle and trapezoid methods.

We now calculate an approximation using the trapezoid method for $\cos(x)$ between $-\pi/2$ and $\pi/2$ with up to 41 subintervals.

❑ [A]uthor `vector([i,trapezoid_sum(`

`cosx,x,-pi/2,pi/2,i)],i,1,41,4)` $\boxed{\hookleftarrow}$

appro$\boxed{\mathrm{X}}$ $\boxed{\hookleftarrow}$

#8:
$$\begin{bmatrix} 1 & 0 \\ 5 & 1.93376 \\ 9 & 1.97965 \\ 13 & 1.99025 \\ 17 & 1.99430 \\ 21 & 1.99626 \\ 25 & 1.99736 \\ 29 & 1.99804 \\ 33 & 1.99848 \\ 37 & 1.99879 \\ 41 & 1.99902 \end{bmatrix}$$

With the decomposition into 41 trapezoids the error is less that one thousandth.

We now go on to use the limit command and compare this with the integral calculation.

❑ $\boxed{\text{A}}$uthor `trapezoid_sum(cosx,x,-pi/2,pi/2,n)` $\boxed{\hookleftarrow}$

$\boxed{\text{C}}$alculus $\boxed{\text{L}}$imit $\boxed{\hookleftarrow}$ variable: n $\boxed{\hookleftarrow}$ Point: inf $\boxed{\hookleftarrow}$

$\boxed{\text{S}}$implify $\boxed{\hookleftarrow}$

#9: $\text{TRAPEZOID\_SUM}\left[\cos(x),\ x,\ -\dfrac{\pi}{2},\ \dfrac{\pi}{2},\ n\right]$

#10: $\lim\limits_{n\to\infty} \text{TRAPEZOID\_SUM}\left[\cos(x),\ x,\ -\dfrac{\pi}{2},\ \dfrac{\pi}{2},\ n\right]$

#11: 2

❑ $\boxed{\text{A}}$uthor `cosx` $\boxed{\hookleftarrow}$

$\boxed{\text{C}}$alculus $\boxed{\text{I}}$ntegrate $\boxed{\hookleftarrow}$ variable: x $\boxed{\hookleftarrow}$

Lower limit: `-pi/2` $\boxed{\leftrightarrows}$ Upper limit: `pi/2` $\boxed{\hookleftarrow}$

$\boxed{\text{S}}$implify $\boxed{\hookleftarrow}$

#12: $\cos(x)$

#13: $\displaystyle\int_{-\pi/2}^{\pi/2} \cos(x)\ dx$

#14: 2

Here the calculation of the indefinite integral using the limit command also works.

❑ $\boxed{\text{A}}$uthor `trapezoid_sum(cosx,x,a,b,n)` $\boxed{\hookleftarrow}$

$\boxed{\text{C}}$alculus $\boxed{\text{L}}$imit $\boxed{\hookleftarrow}$ variable: n $\boxed{\hookleftarrow}$ Point: inf $\boxed{\hookleftarrow}$

$\boxed{\text{S}}$implify $\boxed{\hookleftarrow}$

#15: $\text{TRAPEZOID\_SUM}(\cos(x),\ x,\ a,\ b,\ n)$

#16: $\lim\limits_{n\to\infty} \text{TRAPEZOID\_SUM}(\cos(x),\ x,\ a,\ b,\ n)$

#17: $\sin(b) - \sin(a)$

And once again the same calculation performed using integration.

❑ [A]uthor cosx [↵]

    [C]aluclus [I]ntegrate [↵] variable: x [↵]

        Lower limit: a [⇆] Upper limit: b [↵]

    [S]implify [↵]

```
#18: COS(x)

        b
#19: ∫   COS(x) dx
     a

#20: SIN(b) - SIN(a)
```

It can and will always happen that while using a computer, a student may require help, not knowing what to do next. Or one may find oneself in the same situation: there is some image on the screen and the computer does not react at all as expected. It is often too complex, if not completely impossible to know why, or even how, the user came to this situation. In this situation the teacher is like a doctor who must determine the illness and treatment of a patient from a couple of symptoms.

In this chapter we have collected several such problems with the cooperation of many DERIVE users, mostly teachers throughout Europe. Every example that is not from the author is annotated with the name of the person responsible for it.

Not only are the examples handy for those panic cases where nothing works as it should, but they also act to clarify the finer details of the system. The tips are therefore not without value for the experienced user.

We describe the symptoms and give one or more solutions to each problem. We have arranged the problems in groups:

- Input of Expressions
- Expression Manipulation
- Vectors and Matrices
- Function Evaluation
- Solving Equations
- Plotting Graphs
- Loading and Saving

Input of expressions

⊗ The use of variable names with more then one letter can lead to incomprehensible results:

    ⌊A⌋uthor 2 apples + 3 apples ⏎

$\boxed{\text{S}}$implify $\boxed{\hookleftarrow}$

```
#1:   2·a·p·p·l·e·s + 3·a·p·p·l·e·s

            2
#2:   5·a·e·l·p ·s
```

☺ The default is to allow only single letter variable names. This is sufficient for most purposes and allows more simple input. For instance 'xy' for the product of x and y (i.e. one doesn't need to input the multiplication sign) or 'sinx' for the sine of the variable x (i.e. one can often ignore parentheses). If the user would prefer to work with longer variable names, one must change the input mode from Character to Word:

```
OPTIONS INPUT: Mode: Character Word  Case:(Insensitive)Sensitive
               Use:(LineEdit)Subexpression
```

☹ Inputting $\sin x$ leads to an unexpected result.

$\boxed{\text{A}}$uthor sinx $\boxed{\hookleftarrow}$

$\boxed{\text{S}}$implify $\boxed{\hookleftarrow}$

```
#2:   s·i·n·x

#3:   i·n·s·x
```

☺ The currently selected input mode

```
OPTIONS INPUT: Mode:(Character)Word  Case: Insensitive Sensitive
               Use:(LineEdit)Subexpression
```

distinguishes between upper and lower case, so that the sine function, internally known as SIN, is not recognised. Either one must observe the case:

$\boxed{\text{A}}$uthor SINx $\boxed{\hookleftarrow}$

or we need to change the case sensitivity setting:

$\boxed{\text{O}}$ptions $\boxed{\text{I}}$nput $\boxed{\leftarrow}$ Case: $\boxed{\text{I}}$nsensitive

(S. Cappuccio, Forli)

☹ Does one actually need to use the ›Author‹ command 5 times in order to make 5 assignments?

☺ No. One can write the 5 assignments as a vector, e.g.:

$\boxed{\text{A}}$uthor [a1:=1,a2:=2,a3:=1.5,a4:=7,a5:=1] $\boxed{\hookleftarrow}$

(P. Mitic, Hampshire)

☻ How can the value of a variable or the definition of a function be erased?

☺ When *f* is the name of a variable containing a value, or the name of a user-defined function, then both can be erased using:

    ⌐A⌐uthor f:=f ⌐↵⌐

f is then a variable without content.

☻ A syntax error occurs during the input of a variable, e.g.:

```
AUTHOR expression: f_

Syntax error detected at cursor
```

☺ There is probably already a function with the name *f*, so the system expects an opening parenthesis at the cursor position. If the function is no longer needed, then it should be erased before this expression is input. Otherwise one must select another variable name.

☻ A syntax error occurs during the input of an assignment, e.g.:

```
AUTHOR expression: rate:=250

Syntax error detected at cursor
```

☺ RATE is a reserved word for a financial function. One must select another variable name, e.g.:

    ⌐A⌐uthor monthlyrate:=250 ⌐↵⌐

(P. Mitic, Hampshire)

☻ A syntax error occurs during the input of a function application, e.g.:

```
AUTHOR expression: f(1,2)

Syntax error detected at cursor
```

☺ The function is unknown, being neither a built-in nor a user-defined function. Only known functions may be input, except in the event that we are defining a function. In this case an unknown function may (should) be on the left hand side of the assignment operator ':='. It is often the case that the reason for this problem is a simple misspelling.

☻ A syntax error occurs during the input of an expression, e.g.:

```
AUTHOR expression: x/(x+√(1-x^2)_

Syntax error detected at cursor
```

☺ In this case the number of opening brackets is different to the number of closing brackets.

☹ Through a change of the screen controls, the screen becomes unreadable.

☺ From the following five suggestions, only the first two keep the current data.
  • Make a blind switch to Text mode, which is readable on practically every screen.

[ESC] [ESC] [ESC] [ESC]   (To guarantee that we are in the main menu)
[O]ptions [D]isplay [T]ext [↵]

  • Reload the system initialisation file DERIVE.INI:

[ESC] [ESC] [ESC] [ESC]   (To guarantee that we are in the main menu)
[T]ransfer [L]oad [S]tate [↵]

  • Exit DERIVE:

[ESC] [ESC] [ESC] [ESC]   (To guarantee that we are in the main menu)
[Q]uit y [↵]

  • Give the "Three-finger-salute" [STRG]-[ALT]-[ENTF].
  • Do a hard restart, but only if all else fails.

(S. Biryukov, Moscow)

Expression manipulation

☹ Complex numbers don't work as expected.

[A]uthor (2+3i)(1-i) = [↵]

```
#1:  (2 + 3·i)·(1 - i) = (1 - i)·(3·i + 2)
```

☺ The imaginary unit has been falsely entered; it is not written simply 'i', rather as '#i' or '[ALT]-[I]'. On the screen it is written with a circumflex in order to distinguish it from the variable i .

[A]uthor (2+3#i)(1-#i) = [↵]

```
#2:  (2 + 3·î)·(1 - î) = 5 + î
```

☹ The differential of e^x (or any other operation performed upon e^x) doesn't work as expected.

[A]uthor dif(e^x,x) = [↵]

$$\text{\#4:} \quad \frac{d}{dx} e^x = e^x \cdot \text{LN}(e)$$

☺ The constant *e* above is not input as 'e', rather as '#e' or 'ALT-E'. On the screen it is written with a circumflex in order to distinguish it from the variable *e*.

[A]uthor dif(#e^x,x) = [↵]

$$\text{\#5:} \quad \frac{d}{dx} \hat{e}^x = \hat{e}^x$$

☹ A simplification returns a too general, thus incorrect, result.

[A]uthor x>-1 and x>-2 [↵]

[S]implify [↵]

#4: x > -1 AND x > -2

#5: true

☺ The range of one or more variables is defined so that the seemingly false general answer is indeed the most correct one. In the above example, *x* is declared as a positive integer, thus the answer is correct.

☹ The following expression is not simplified to zero:

[A]uthor √(xy) - √x√y [↵]

[S]implify

#1: $\sqrt{(x \cdot y)} - \sqrt{x} \cdot \sqrt{y}$

#2: $\sqrt{(x \cdot y)} - \sqrt{x} \cdot \sqrt{y}$

☺ The expression is not in fact equivalent to zero. If we replace *x* and *y* with -1 we see:

#3: $\sqrt{((-1) \cdot (-1))} - \sqrt{(-1)} \cdot \sqrt{(-1)}$

#4: 2

If one uses the ›Declare‹ command to force at least one of the variables to be non-negative, then DERIVE will simplify the expression to zero.

☹ The expression $(a+b)^2$ is not simplified to $a^2 +2ab+b^2$.

☺ At least one of a and b is probably still assigned a value from an earlier assignment. Clear the assignment and simplify the expression again.

☹ The simplification of an expression returns an unexpected decimal, e.g. $1/2 + 1/3$ simplifies to 0.833333 instead of 5/6.

☺ One of the following settings is likely to be the problem:

- `OPTIONS PRECISION: Mode: `**`Approximate`**` Exact Mixed  Digits: 6`

- `OPTIONS PRECISION: Mode: Approximate Exact `**`Mixed`**`  Digits: 6`

- `OPTIONS NOTATION: Style: `**`Decimal`**` Mixed Rational Scientific  Digits: 6`

- `OPTIONS NOTATION: Style: Decimal Mixed Rational `**`Scientific`**`  Digits: 6`

☹ The calculation of very high index members of a sequence gives the wrong answer.

[A]uthor `f(x):=(1+1/x)^x` [↵]

[A]uthor `vector(f(x),x,100000,500000,100000)` [↵]

appro[X] [↵]

```
#1:  F(x) := [1 + 1/x]^x

#2:  VECTOR(F(x), x, 100000, 500000, 100000)

#3:  [1, 1, 1, 1, 1]
```

☺ The false answer comes through rounding errors. Raising the accuracy to, say, 10 places and applying ›approX‹ once again gives:

```
#4:  PrecisionDigits := 10

#5:  [2.718268199, 2.718275032, 2.718277298, 2.718278430, 2.718279110]
```

(A. Garcia, A. Martinez, R. Minano, F. Rincón, Madrid)

⊗ After a successful calculation DERIVE shows the calculation time:

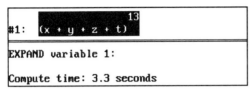

but before the result appears on the screen, an error message appears:

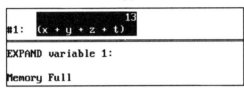

☺ DERIVE has enough memory to perform the calculation, but not enough to format and display the result. The following solutions might work:
- Erase all unnecessary expressions and attempt the calculation again.
- If you are using DERIVE CLASSIC then there is only 640 KB memory available. If you have a more powerful machine, for instance a PC-386, -486, or -Pentium with at least 2 MB main memory, then the example could be solved using DERIVE PROFESSIONAL.

⊗ When one uses the ›Manage Substitute‹ command to replace t^3 with k in $\sin(t^3) + t^6 + t^3$, an unexpected answer is returned:

Mark the subexpression t^3.

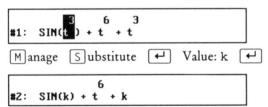

How can one ensure that t^6 is replaced with k^2?

☺ The substitution command replaces only those subexpressions that match the chosen expression exactly. Instead of replacing t^3 with k, one should replace t with $k^{1/3}$.

⎡M⎤anage ⎡S⎤ubstitute expression: #1 ⎡↵⎤ ... replace 't' with 'k^(1/3)' ⎡↵⎤
⎡S⎤implify ⎡↵⎤

$$\text{\#3: } \text{SIN}((k^{1/3})^3) + (k^{1/3})^6 + (k^{1/3})^3$$

$$\text{\#4: } \text{SIN}(k) + k^2 + k$$

(D. Stoutemyer, Honolulu)

Vectors and matrices

☹ The following calculation of the determinant of a matrix gives another matrix:

[A]uthor det([[a,4],[5,b]]) [↵]

[S]implify [↵]

$$\text{\#2: } \text{DET} \begin{bmatrix} a & 4 \\ 5 & b \end{bmatrix}$$

$$\text{\#3: } \begin{bmatrix} 3 \cdot b - 20 & 4 \cdot b \\ 5 \cdot b & 6 \cdot b - 20 \end{bmatrix}$$

☺ The variable *a* was previously assigned a matrix, so the result is correct:

$$\text{\#1: } a := \begin{bmatrix} 3 & 4 \\ 5 & 6 \end{bmatrix}$$

One must clear the assignment of *a* and simplify the expression once again.

[A]uthor a:=a [↵]

[S]implify #2 [↵]

$$\text{\#4: } a := a$$

$$\text{\#5: } a \cdot b - 20$$

(A. Garcia, A. Martinez, R. Minano, F. Rincón, Madrid)

☹ The attempt to carry out the following multiplication using the ›Simplify‹ command fails.

$$\text{\#3: } \begin{bmatrix} 1 \\ 2 \\ 3 \end{bmatrix} \cdot [x, y, z]$$

☺ The left factor is a matrix, while the right factor is a vector (recognisable by the commas between the elements). One must turn the vector into a matrix as follows. Copy the expression with ⌈F3⌉ into the input line.

```
AUTHOR expression: [[1], [2], [3]] · [x, y, z]_
```

Enter an extra pair of square brackets:

```
AUTHOR expression: [[1], [2], [3]] ·[[x, y, z]]
```

The right factor is now written (see expression #5) without commas, indicating that it is now a matrix. Simplification now gives the desired result.

$$
\#5: \quad \begin{bmatrix} 1 \\ 2 \\ 3 \end{bmatrix} \cdot [\, x \quad y \quad z \,]
$$

$$
\#6: \quad \begin{bmatrix} x & y & z \\ 2 \cdot x & 2 \cdot y & 2 \cdot z \\ 3 \cdot x & 3 \cdot y & 3 \cdot z \end{bmatrix}
$$

(A. Garcia, A. Martinez, R. Minano, F. Rincón, Madrid)

☒ How can one input a column vector $\begin{pmatrix} a \\ b \end{pmatrix}$?

☺ There are two possibilities. One can use matrix notation, writing the column vector as a matrix with rows containing only one element,

Ａuthor [[a], [b]] ⌈↵⌋

$$
\#1: \quad \begin{bmatrix} a \\ b \end{bmatrix}
$$

or we can transpose a row vector.

Ａuthor [a,b]`= ⌈↵⌋

$$
\#2: \quad [a, b]` = \begin{bmatrix} a \\ b \end{bmatrix}
$$

(S. Cappuccio, Forli)

Function evaluation

☹ The following expression cannot be calculated with ›Simplify‹ nor with ›approX‹:

$$\#1:\quad \text{FIT}\left[[x, a \cdot x + b], \begin{bmatrix} 1 & 2 \\ 3 & 4 \end{bmatrix}\right]$$

☺ During input of the expression, square, instead of round brackets, were used for the arguments for FIT. Copying this expression into the input line one sees that there are too many square brackets:

```
AUTHOR expression: FIT([[x, a·x + b], [[1, 2], [3, 4]]])
```

The input should have been:

Ⓐuthor fit([x,ax+b],[[1,2],[3,4]]) [↵]

and is displayed:

$$\#2:\quad \text{FIT}\left[[x, a \cdot x + b], \begin{bmatrix} 1 & 2 \\ 3 & 4 \end{bmatrix}\right]$$

The difference between expressions #1 and #2 is the extra space directly after the FIT function name. Only when there is no space there do we have a proper function call. This sort of error occurs most often when input is taken directly from a DERIVE screen. Since there are no round brackets in the extended ASCII set, DERIVE must use large square brackets where it needs large round brackets.

☹ Using the FIT function to calculate an interpolation polynomial (i.e. the parameterised expression is a polynomial of degree n while the data matrix has $n+1$ points) results in a polynomial that does not go through the points, e.g.:

Ⓐuthor h(x):=(x^2-2)/7-3.3sin(2x) [↵]

Ⓐuthor

vector([x,h(x)],x,[1.3,1.75,2.3,2.7,3.3,3.95,4.75]) [↵]

Ⓢimplify [↵]

Ⓐuthor fit([x,ax^6+bx^5+cx^4+dx^3+ex^2+fx+g],#3) [↵]

Ⓢimplify [↵]

Plot the data matrix and the interpolation polynomial.

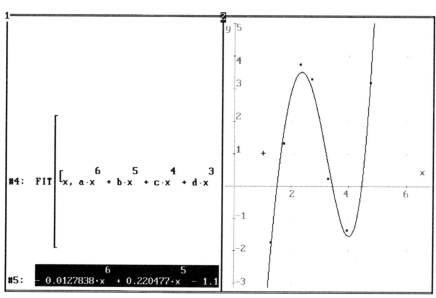

#4: FIT $\left[x, a \cdot x^6 + b \cdot x^5 + c \cdot x^4 + d \cdot x^3 \right.$

#5: $- 0.0127838 \cdot x^6 + 0.220477 \cdot x^5 - 1.1$

☺ The cause is rounding errors. As a rule of thumb, the precision should be set to three more digits than the degree of the polynomial.

(A. Rich, Honolulu)

☹ An indefinite integral simplifies to an expression that has nothing to do with the original function.

#2: $\int x \, dx$

#3: $2 \cdot a^2$

☺ The integration variable has probably been assigned a value elsewhere. This was the case above:

A̅uthor x= ↵

#4: $x = 2 \cdot a$

☹ The calculation of an integral does not give the known answer.

☺ Usually one of the following applies:
  • The result is equivalent to the known answer, just written differently.
  • The results differs only in an added constant.
  • The known answer is only reached by restricting the range of the variable, e.g.:

⬚A⬚uthor int(1/(2-u^2+v^2),v) ⬚↵⬚

⬚S⬚implify ⬚↵⬚

$$
\#1: \quad \int \frac{1}{2 - u^2 + v^2}\, dv
$$

$$
\#2: \quad \frac{LN\left[\dfrac{v - \sqrt{(u^2 - 2)}}{\sqrt{(u^2 - 2)} + v}\right]}{2 \cdot \sqrt{(u^2 - 2)}}
$$

Restrict *u* to the interval between 0 and 1.

⬚D⬚eclare ⬚V⬚ariable u ⬚↵⬚   ⬚R⬚eal ⬚I⬚nterval

Change the limits of integration as follows:

```
DECLARE VARIABLE: Bounds: 0          <(≤) u   <(≤) 1_
```

Calculate the integral once again.

⬚S⬚implify #1 ⬚↵⬚

#3: u :∈ Real [0, 1]

$$
\#4: \quad \frac{ATAN\left[\dfrac{v}{\sqrt{(2 - u^2)}}\right]}{\sqrt{(2 - u^2)}}
$$

(J. Wiesenbauer, Vienna)

⊗ When the first derivative of the function f is assigned the name $f1$ in the following way:

⬚A⬚uthor f1(x):=dif(f(x),x) ⬚↵⬚

then the attempt to calculate the derivative at a point fails.

⬚A⬚uthor f1(2)= ⬚↵⬚

$$
\#3: \quad F1(2) = \frac{d}{d2}\, F(2)
$$

☺ The assignment of the name ƒ1 should be carried out as follows:

[A]uthor `dif(f(x),x)` [↵]

[S]implify [↵]

[A]uthor `f1(x) :=` [F3]

(W. Obereder, Berndorf)

☻ If a variable is used to call the random number generator, then the laws of arithmetic do not apply to this variable anymore. For example $2x$ differs from $x + x$:

[A]uthor `x:=random(6)+1` [↵]

[A]uthor `x+x=2x` [↵]

[S]implify [↵]

[S]implify `#2` [↵]

[S]implify `#2` [↵]

```
#1:  x := RANDOM(6) + 1

#2:  x + x = 2·x

#3:  6 = 10

#4:  10 = 10

#5:  7 = 6
```

☺ In the expression $x + x$ the random number generator is called twice, so that it is the sum of two random numbers. For $2x$ the random number generator is called only once and the result is doubled. Obviously these results agree only by chance.

☻ When one simplifies the expression

```
      100
#1:    Σ   RANDOM(2)
      k=1
```

the result is not numbers around the expected value of this experiment, but rather exclusively 0 or 100.

> #2: $\left[\sum_{k=1}^{100} \text{RANDOM(2)}, \quad \sum_{k=1}^{100} \text{RANDOM(2)}, \quad \sum_{k=1}^{100} \right.$
>
> #3: [0, 0, 100, 0, 100, 0]

☺ The application of the ›Simplify‹ command calculates a solution to the symbolic problem $\sum_{k=1}^{n} x$, namely nx, and then replaces x and n with the values RANDOM(2) and 100. In order to sum 100 random 0-1 experiments, one must apply the ›approX‹ command.

> #4: [53, 47, 51, 54, 43, 54]

(J. Wiesenbauer, Vienna)

Solving equations

☹ One solves a system of equations with the SOLVE function and then attempts to find the first solution using the ELEMENT or SUB functions without success:

[A]uthor `solve([x+y=1,x-y=1],[x,y])` [↵]

[S]implify [↵]

[A]uthor [F3] `sub 1=` [↵]

> #5: $[x = 1 \quad y = 0] = [x = 1, y = 0]$
>   1

☺ A second application of the ELEMENT or SUB function will bring out the solution. The reason is that the SOLVE function returns the result as a one-rowed matrix, not as a vector. The first application thus gives the first (and only) row vector. This is seen in the above by the appearance of a comma in the right hand expression but not in the left.

(J. Lechner, Amstetten)

☺ The solving of a system of nonlinear equations results in an empty list.

[A]uthor `solve([x^2+y^2=1,x-y=1],[x,y])` [↵]

[S]implify [↵]

> #1: $\text{SOLVE}([x^2 + y^2 = 1, x - y = 1], [x, y])$
>
> #2: []

☺ SOLVE and the ›soLve‹ command can only solve linear systems of equations. Nonlinear systems have to be transformed manually, step by step.

⊗ An attempt to solve the system $x + y + z = 2$, $x + y - z = 8$ for x and y, ends with the message:

No solutions found

If one solves the system for x and z, then the following answer appears:

#2:   [x = 5 - y, z = -3]

☺ If a system of equations has fewer equations than variables, the solution can depend on the selected variables. This can be avoided by adding trivial equations such as 0=0 to the system so that there are as many equations as variables before invoking the ›soLve‹ command or applying the SOLVE function.

#3:   [x + y + z = 2, x + y - z = 8, 0 = 0]
#4:   [x = @1, y = 5 - @1, z = -3]

(A. Garcia, A. Martinez, R. Minano, F. Rincón, Madrid)

Plotting graphs

⊗ After invoking the ›Plot‹ command a collection of points appears on the screen instead of the chosen graph.

☺ The screen mode must be set to Graphics:

[O]ptions   [D]isplay

Mode: Text **Graphics** Reso: Medium(High) Text:(Large)Small Set: Std(Extended) Adapter: MDA CGA EGA MCGA(VGA)Hercules AT&T T3100 95LX PCjr Other

⊗ The graph of $\sin x$ is a 45° line.

☺ Probably word mode is set, so that variable names are allowed to be arbitrarily long, and 'sinx' has been typed in. In this mode, this input has been interpreted as a variable with the four letter name 'sinx'. Either one must type 'sin(x)', or the input must be set to character mode and 'sinx' entered once again.

OPTIONS INPUT: Mode: Character **Word** Case:(Insensitive)Sensitive   Use:(LineEdit)Subexpression

⊗ The graph of $\sin x$ is a horizontal line.

☺ The variable x has been assigned a value. Either clear this assignment or use a different variable.

(S. Townend, D. Pountney, Liverpool)

☹ The graph of an expression seems to be a mirror image. For example x is drawn as a 135°-line or the point (1/1) is placed at (1/−1).

☺ Probably one of the following applies:

- A previous assignment has taken place, e.g.:

```
#2:  x := -y
```

- One of the axis units has a negative scale value, e.g.:

```
SCALE: x: 1                    y: -1
```

☹ Invoking the ›Plot‹ command has no effect.

☺ There are many possible causes, e.g.:
- The graph doesn't exist in the real number plane.
- The graph doesn't lie within the plot frame.
- The colour of the graph is the same as the background colour.

The following measures can help alleviate the problem:
- Evaluate the expression at some point to ensure that it really does have a real part, and that it falls in the plot frame.
- Change the plot frame using the ›Range‹, ›Zoom‹, ›Center‹ or ›Scale‹ commands, or use the keys [F7], [F8], [F9] or [F10].
- Use the automatic scaling of the y-axis. It is turned on by the command: [S]cale [⇆] Auto: [Y]es.

☹ How can one plot the graph of $y = f(x)$ only for a specific interval, independent of the plot frame?

☺ One writes the graph as a parameterised graph $[x, f(x)]$, and gives the interval in for the parameter limits, e.g.:

[A]uthor [x,lnx] [↵]

[P]lot [B]eside [↵]

[P]lot

```
PLOT: Min: -3.14159   Max: 3.14159   Mode:(Continuous)Discrete  Points: 20
```

Min: 0.5 [⇆] Max: 1.5 [↵]

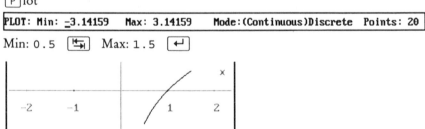

(J. Wiesenbauer, Vienna)

☻ Invoking the ›Plot‹ command on a family of functions has no effect:

[A]uthor vector(ax^2,a,-2,2,.25) [↵]

```
                 2
#1:  VECTOR(a·x , a, -2, 2, 0.25)
```

[P]lot [B]eside [↵]
[P]lot

☺ The expression must be simplified before it is plotted with ›Plot‹.

[S]implify [↵]
[P]lot [P]lot

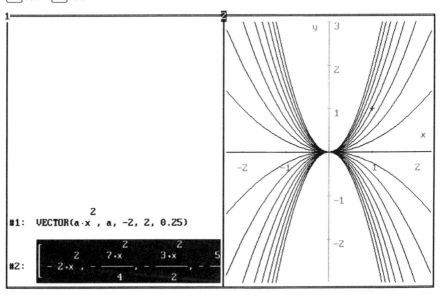

(S. Cappuccio, Forli)

☻ How can two expressions $f(x)$ and $g(x)$ be plotted using a single ›Plot‹ command? If they are written as entries in a vector, DERIVE interprets them as the x and y coordinates of a parameterised curve, which is not intended.

☺ Put $f(x)$ and $g(x)$ in a three-element list with a (graphically) meaningless third element:

[A]uthor [f(x),g(x),?] [↵]

☹ When working in trace mode, the graphic-box leaves the screen.

☺ Probably the user has (inadvertently) pressed one of the ⎡↑⎤ or ⎡↓⎤ keys and the graphics-box has jumped to a curve that is lying outside the plot frame. Check on the lower left part of the screen which expression is currently being traced, and where it is. Use the ›Move‹ command to bring the graphics-box back on screen.

☹ When working in trace mode, either ⎡↑⎤ or ⎡↓⎤ is used to move to a different curve, and the whole plot frame moves.

☺ The follow cross mode is switched on

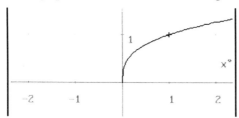

and the graphics-box has moved to a curve that lies outside the plot frame (the x-coordinate remains constant). The follow cross mode ensures that the plot frame follows the graphics-box.

☹ By the graph of $x^{1/3}$ the branch with negative values of x are not drawn:

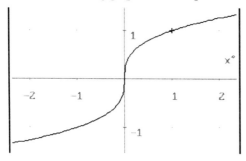

☺ In DERIVE it can be decided which root will be used. The default is to use the principal root, i.e. the root with the lowest phase angle. If the real roots should be used, the default must be changed:

MANAGE BRANCH: Principal Real Any

Then the following graph of $x^{1/3}$ is plotted:

☻ When in trace mode one of the graphs is not reachable, for example, the lowest in this example:

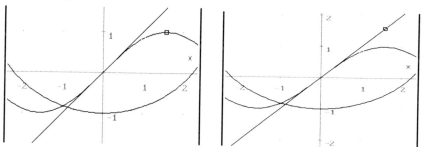

☺ This graph is implicitly defined (expression #3) and is thus not reachable in trace mode.

```
#1:  SIN(x)

#2:  x

       2          2
#3:  x  + (y - 2)  = 9
```

☹ In trace mode the picture is repeatedly zoomed. The graphics-box leaves the plotted graph and cannot be brought back with the [↑] or [↓] keys.

☺ The unit length of the axes has decreased to be of the same order as the precision of calculation, so that rounding errors become visible. To remedy this, the plot accuracy must be increased and the graph re-plotted.

☹ By repeatedly zooming a smooth curve the following appears:

☺ This is also a rounding error effect. The plot accuracy must be increased and the graph re-plotted.

For those who are interested, this example deals with the neighbourhood of the maximum in the following expression:

$$\#3: \quad \frac{4 \cdot x^4 - 59 \cdot x^3 + 324 \cdot x^2 - 751 \cdot x + 622}{x^4 - 14 \cdot x^3 + 72 \cdot x^2 - 151 \cdot x + 112}$$

(D. Stoutemyer, Honolulu)

☹ The plotting of $\sin x$ with the axis scale 'x:20 y:1' produces the following:

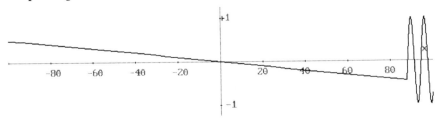

☺ The plot accuracy is set too low:

```
OPTIONS ACCURACY: 6

Enter plot accuracy (0 to 9)
```

Increasing the value to at least 7 solves the problem.

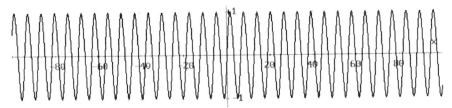

(A. Garcia, A. Martinez, R. Minano, F. Rincón, Madrid)

☹ How can the surface y^2 be plotted as a three dimensional surface? Using

 [P]lot [B]eside [↵]

 [P]lot

 produces the standard two-dimensional picture of a parabola.

☺ Use the expression $y^2 + 0 \cdot x$ and plot as usual.

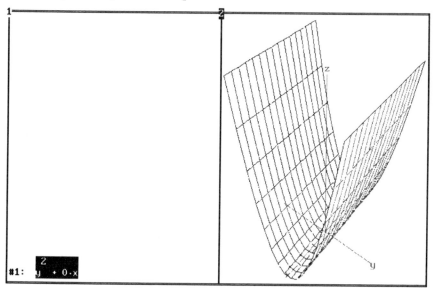

Alternatively we can plot y^2 three dimensionally by explicitly opening a 3D Graphics window in advance:

 [W]indow [S]plit [V]ertical [↵]

 [F1] (to move to the right window)

 [W]indow [D]esignate [3]D-plot y

(S. Cappuccio, Forli)

Loading and saving

☹ While carrying out a Load command, e.g.:

 [T]ransfer [L]oad [D]erive

 a warning tone is heard and a line is not read.

☺ In this line there is an application of an unknown function. Before the file can be correctly read, the function must be properly defined.

⊗ When the number π is approximated with the ›approX‹ command, expression #2 results.

```
#1:  π

#2:  3.14159
```

When expressions #1 and #2 are saved with ›Transfer Save Derive‹ in a file and then loaded with ›Transfer Load Derive‹, the following appears:

```
#1:  π

         355
#2:  ─────
         113
```

☺ The reason for this lies with the fact that approximations are internally made with fractions, using the so-called Matula arithmetic. Thus expression #2 is internally a fraction that is written in decimal form as a side effect of the ›approX‹ command. When the expression is saved and reloaded this side effect falls away and a fraction is printed, depending upon the default setting:

```
OPTIONS NOTATION: Style: Decimal Mixed Rational Scientific  Digits: 6
```

If we changed the default, then we would read every fraction as a decimal, something we probably don't want. Instead of this, before saving we can copy expression #2 to expression #3 using [F3]:

[A]uthor pi [↵]

appro[X] [↵]

[A]uthor [F3] [↵]

```
#1:  π

#2:  3.14159

#3:  3.14159
```

If these expressions are saved and reloaded, one gets:

```
#1:  π

         355
#2:  ─────
         113

#3:  3.14159
```

(A. Garcia, A. Martinez, R. Minano, F. Rincón, Madrid)

CHAPTER 6

YOUR OWN SYSTEM: USER-DEFINED MENUS

DERIVE Version 3 introduces a valuable feature for teaching: the complete menu system is user configurable. For practical use in teaching the following possibilities arise:

- Commands can be given new names
- Commands can be made inaccessible
- Commands can be moved

This feature is undocumented in the manual. That is unfortunate, but also an opportunity for us to let you in on the secret.

Sometimes one is dissatisfied with the command word selected by the software producer (or translator). Regardless of whether this is due to personal preference or as a result of local tradition; the ability to change the names of commands and their activation letters is enough for most people. However, the choice is not completely free; the complete menu must fit into two lines and the activation letter must be unique for each command in the menu. Perhaps one doesn't like the ›Author‹ command name, and would rather it were called ›Write‹ This would be fine, except that the letter W is used for the ›Window‹ command. In fact the only available letter is "I", so we would have to use ›wrIte‹.

In the case of the Scaffolding, the commands and functions should be introduced to the students slowly. If we were looking at the solution of equations, then the ›Simplify‹ command should be available, but not the ›soLve‹ command. Some teachers feel that it is sufficient to teach the correct methods to the students, believing that cheating hurts only the student herself and that self-discipline should be a part of the learning process. And anyway, a copy of the solution process, either on disk or on paper, could be turned in as homework. Others feel that it is better not to lead students into temptation, and to keep the unnecessary commands out of reach. Both types of teaching method, and all variations thereupon, can be accomodated.

Sometimes there is a command on a second level of menus that is repeatedly needed, and it would be preferable to bring this to the top level menu (The ›Manage Substitute‹ command is such an example). With user-defined menus this can be achieved, the levels of the menu hierarchy can be arbitrarily modified.

Thus it is possible to make a menu system for each level of schooling, providing a custom tailored computer algebra tool for each class of user. The modification of the menu system is as simple as described in the sequel.

A user defined menu system is saved in a file called DERIVE.MEN. When invoking the system, it is checked to see if a file with this name is in the current directory, in the \DERIVE directory or in the home directory from which DERIVE was started. If not, then the original menu system is used. Alternatively, one can choose any file name with the extension .MEN. In this case one would have to specify the menu system file name after the `derive` command, e.g. 'derive deri1.men'.

DERIVE.MEN is an ASCII text file. The contents are essentially a translation table between the new menu system and the original. Let's first cast our gaze over an example for a translation into German, to see the gross structure. The first few lines could be:

```
(("Schreibe" "Author")
 ("Vereinfache" "Simplify")
 ("Löse" "soLve")
 ("Mult" "Expand")
 ("faKt" "Factor")
 ("approX" "approX")
 ..... )
```

From this we can observe the following rules:

- A menu is written as a sequence of bracketed expressions, positioned between an outer pair of brackets.
- Every bracketed expression refers to a single menu command.
- Inside each bracketed expression we see first the new command word, in quotation marks, then the original command word, also in quotes.

- In both the new and old command words there is exactly one capital letter, that being the one that activates the command.
- In all the new command words together, no capital letter may be repeated.

This is enough to prepare a tiny main menu for a "Minimal-DERIVE".

❑ With an editor, create an ASCII text file called `deriv1.men` containing the following:

```
( ("Write" "Author")
  ("Simplify" "Simplify")
  ("suBstitute" "Manage" "Substitute")
  ("End" "Quit") )
```

In this example we see two more rules:

- If a command is a result of two (or more) command words in sequence, then these are to be written in (the same) sequence, but with each individual command word in quotes.
- Every main menu must have a command to quit DERIVE , for example ›End‹ ›sTop‹ or ›Quit‹.

If one starts DERIVE with this menu, then it looks like:

❑ `derive deriv1.men`

```
COMMAND: Write Simplify suBstitute End

Enter option
                              Free:100%           Derive Algebra
```

Now to a submenu. First, let's look at an example from the German translation file:

```
. . . . .
  ("Baue"  "Build")
  ("Def"
      ("Funktion" "Declare" "Function")
      ("Variable" "Declare" "Variable")
      ("Matrix" "Declare" "Matrix")
      ("veKtor" "Declare" "vectoR")          )
. . . . .
```

From this we see the following rules:

- A submenu is also a sequence of bracketed expressions.
- The submenu comes in the space that, in the rules above, would be taken by the original command word.

This suffices to extend the above mini main menu with a submenu.

❑ Insert the following before the last closing bracket:

```
("End"  "Quit")
("sUbmenu"
         ("Approximate"  "approX")
         ("Solve"  "soLve")
         ("Differentiate"  "Calculus"  "Differentiate")  )
       )
```

It is very important not to forget a bracket, since if one does, the computer will freeze up. In particular the second closing bracket directly after "Differentiate" is to be noted. It closes the ›sUbmenu‹ expression and is easily forgotten. When we start DERIVE with this new extended menu, and then invoke the ›sUbmenu‹ submenu command, we see:

❑ `derive deriv1.men`

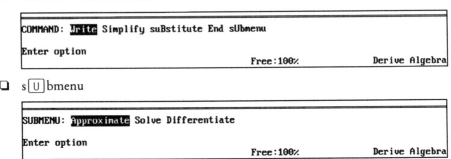

❑ s⎡U⎤bmenu

In the DERIVE.MEN file the following sequence is necessary:

① Algebra Menu
② 2D Graphic Menu
③ 3D Graphic Menu
④ Window Management Menu

CHAPTER 7

HOW DOES A COMPUTER ALGEBRA SYSTEM WORK?

How is computer algebra, that is, algebra carried out by a machine, even possible? How can a computer do something that we thought that only professional mathematicians could do? It is quite bizarre that a computer can not only do symbolic and algebraic computations, but can do them faster and more accurately than any mathematician (even the best miscalculate occasionally).

This phenomenon is not new at all. The standard calculator has capabilities that were until recently regarded as the exclusive province of a few specially trained people. Even something as simple as calculating with numbers was regarded by the Egyptians as a strange mystic skill. In those days the scribes had the extremely responsible job of maintaining all records for the state, whether for the pharaoh's gold or the books in the Library of Alexandria.

In this chapter we look at some mechanisms that every computer algebra system uses as a basis. But first we need to dispel some widespread misconceptions.

A computer algebra system solves problems differently to the way a person would. For those problems that people can calculate, due to their size, the algorithms that we have are about as good as they get. For larger problems they often turn out to be rather inefficient. Since we are most interested in larger problems when dealing with computers, we use those algorithms that work best with larger examples. For smaller examples the difference in efficiency is no longer important, since the efficient algorithm for small examples taking 2/100 of a second is not practically better than the less efficient algorithm taking 9/100 of a second. This is why a computer algebra system cannot easily display the steps of the solution; it could, but the steps are incomprehensible to us.

Some believe that the advantage of computers lies mostly in their speed. Thus people think computers need only use the most basic algorithms, for instance, exhaustive search. Exactly the opposite is the case: one needs better, more intelligent algorithms to achieve better results on dumb but fast hardware (the computer), than one would using intelligent but slow hardware (people). With power, in the sense of speed alone, the computer would not be able to compete at all. Only with the combination of speed and intelligently assembled software can computers manage achievements that begin to compete with humans. Chess computers are a good example. Until very recently even the best chess computers had no chance against a Grandmaster level chess player. Today the picture begins to change: since more and more intelligence is embedded in the programming, computers start to become candidates for the title of World Grandmaster.

The importance of intelligent (read efficient) algorithms can be made clear by the following thought experiment.

Suppose we had two computers to use, the second being 64 times faster than the first. Then suppose we had two algorithms with respective *computational complexity* of 2^n and n^2. (Computational complexity is a measure of the time taken to solve a problem. If an algorithm has a complexity of $f(n)$ then it means for an input of size n we need $f(n)$ units of time to solve the problem. If the size of an input were to be the number of digits in the number, then the input 3876 would have size 4.) Suppose also that we have a total of 2^{20} units of time to spend on the problem, measured on the slower machine. If a time unit was a millisecond, then we have approximately 1050 seconds.

For the first algorithm with a complexity of 2^n we can deal with problems up to $n = 20$ (solving $2^n = 2^{20}$). With the second computer we have 64 times as much time, so solving $2^n = 64.2^{20}$ implies that we can deal with problems up to n=26.

For the second algorithm, with complexity n^2, we can use the first computer for problems up to $n = 1024$, while with the second computer we can go as high as $n = 8,192$, since $2^{26} = 8192^2 = 2^6 \cdot 1024^2 = 2^6 \cdot 2^{20}$, an eightfold increase.

We see that the extra benefit of a computer 64 times faster helps more with the second algorithm, an eightfold increase in capacity as against a 1.3-fold increase for the first algorithm. For this reason we are interested in efficient algorithms.

Now to one of the basic themes of computer algebra.

Arbitrarily long numbers

How can we work with arbitrarily large numbers or arbitrarily long polynomials? From various programming languages we know that there is a largest possible number in a computer and to step over that limit causes a so-called *overflow error*. Furthermore, we can only put so many things in an array or other structure. These limits, learnt in programming courses, have to do with the requirement that we, at some point, define where each object will be found in memory, and how much place it requires.

The following picture represents the memory of a computer. Each memory cell has an address, which we have written in the upper left corner of the cell. It is with this address that the computer internally refers to the memory cell. For simplicity we define a memory cell as the amount of space required to store one number.

#0	#1	#2	#3	#4	#5	#6	#7
#8	#9	#10	#11	#12	#13	#14	#15
#16	#17	#18	#19	#20	#21	#22	#23
#24	#25	#26	#27	#28	#29	#30	#31
#32	#33	#34	#35	#36	#37	#38	#39

Suppose we wanted to work with two arrays $f := [394,213,199]$ and $g := [478,381]$ in a traditional system. Space is allocated in memory for these, perhaps as follows:

#0	#1 394	#2 213	#3 199	#4	#5 478	#6 381	#7
#8	#9	#10	#11	#12	#13	#14	#15
#16	#17	#18	#19	#20	#21	#22	#23
#24	#25	#26	#27	#28	#29	#30	#31
#32	#33	#34	#35	#36	#37	#38	#39

In a table, that could be thought of as an address book, we would find the following:

Variable	Memory Cell
f	1
g	5

The table should be read as follows: the first element of array f is to be found in cell #1, the first element from g in cell #5.

- The advantage of this method lies in the short access times. One can quickly and easily calculate the address of each array element, and thus directly write to or read from the cell. For instance the address of the third element of f is found by adding the address of the first element to the index of the desired element, minus 1. Thus we get cell #3.

- The disadvantage of this method is that an array cannot have more elements than have been allocated to it at the beginning. The above access method will not prevent an attempt to access an array element that does not exist, but nothing sensible will be read, and if a value is written it may interfere with another variable. If one tried to read the sixth element of f, one would get the value of the second element of g, and if one wrote to this address, g would be affected.

This method is termed *static memory management* and is used in most current computer languages.

An alternative to this is the following: instead of dealing with individual memory cells, we pair them together. Arrays become *lists* and are not stored as sequences of values in consecutive cells. Rather, in the first cell-pair we write the first list element in the left cell and in the right cell we write the address of the second cell-pair. In the second cell-pair we write the second list element in the left cell and the address of the third cell-pair in the right cell. This continues until we get to the end of the list, where we write the last element of the list in the left cell of the cell-pair, as usual, and write a keyword in the right cell, usually NIL, to indicate the end of the list.

In this scheme we would put the arrays $f:=[394,213,199]$ and $g:=[478,381]$ into memory as follows:

#0	#1 394	#2 18	#3	#4	#5 478	#6 35	#7
#8		#10	#11	#12	#13	#14	#15
#16	#17	#18 213	#19 30	#20	#21	#22	#23
#24	#25	#26	#27	#28	#29	#30 199	#31 NIL
#32	#33	#34	#35 381	#36 NIL	#37	#38	#39

In the corresponding address table we would see the following:

Variable	Memory Cell
f	1
g	5

The table looks the same as before in that it contains the address of the first memory cell for each array. The fundamental difference lies in the storing of the further list elements. Beforehand the elements were stored consecutively, in this case they are stored arbitrarily, chained together by address references.

- The advantage of this method lies in the arbitrary growth of the list. To add an element to the list just one cell-pair must be found, anywhere in memory. The value is placed in the left cell and the address references are sorted out. A list can thus become as long as the number of cell-pairs that exist in memory.

- The disadvantage of this method is the time it takes for access to individual list elements. To refer to the n-th list element the preceding $n-1$ elements must be scanned through to follow the chain of references.

This method is termed *dynamic memory management* and is the foundation of the programming language LISP. The name derives from the fundamental idea of the language, ›LISt Processing‹. DERIVE is written in the language muLISP, a LISP programming system for PCs.

A number, a polynomial, any expression is represented and manipulated as a list in LISP. The number 1234567890123 would be represented as the list (1,2,3,4,5,6,7,8,9,0,1,2,3).

Working with formulae

How are expressions containing variables dealt with? What is happening behind the scenes when the following dialogue takes place?

❏ [A]uthor (lnx+3)/(ln^2x-9) [↵]

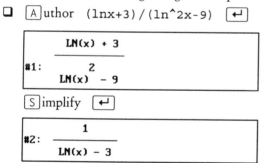

The following discussion derives from David Stoutemyer, one of the authors of DERIVE, and is typical of many computer algebra systems.

Three sub-programs are of interest here, the PARSER, the FORMATTER and the SIMPLIFIER. The symbol string

$$(\ln x + 3) \; / \; (\ln{}^\wedge 2x - 9)$$

received from the user is transformed by the PARSER into the following tree:

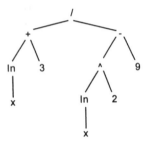

In this representation one sees the syntactic structure of the expression most clearly, whereas the tree is stored internally as a list. If the PARSER comes across some insurmountable barrier, for instance, an extra closing parenthesis, it stops and returns an error message. When all goes well, the FORMATTER takes over, and presents the tree on screen as follows:

$$\frac{LN(x) + 3}{LN(x)^2 - 9}$$

Algorithms for simplification, solving, differentiation, etc. work with the tree representation. When one uses the command ›Simplify‹, the SIMPLIFIER springs onstage and computes, from the tree above, a semantically equivalent but syntactically simpler tree,

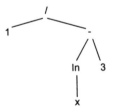

that the FORMATTER then presents as

$$\frac{1}{LN(x) - 3}$$

How the simplification actually takes place in an effective and efficient manner is a (business) secret of those who develop such systems.

Symbolic differentiation

What process is behind the following dialogue?

❑   [A]uthor abx [↵]

[C]alculus [D]ifferentiate [↵] [↵] [↵]

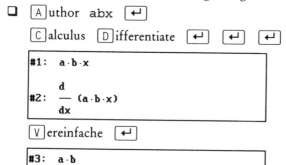

[V]ereinfache [↵]

```
#3:   a · b
```

The command ›Calculus Differentiate‹ has only syntactic importance, applying the built-in function DIF to the input expression. The whole power of symbolic computation is hidden behind the ›Simplify‹ command, which starts by eliminating the DIF function. That is, it finds an expression equivalent to #2 that contains no reference to DIF. In this process DERIVE uses an algorithm in which the well-known rules of derivation are enshrined.

We look at a part of the algorithm, written in easily understood pseudocode.

```
DIF(expression,dif_var):=
        if expression is a number, return 0
        else if expression is a variable
                then if expression=dif_var, return 1
                else return 0
        else if top-level operator of expression is '+'
                return add(DIF(argument1(expression),dif_var),
                                        DIF(argument2(expression),dif_var))
        else if ...
        else if top-level operator of expression is 'SIN'
                return mult(cosine(argument1(expression),
                                        DIF(argument1(expression),dif_var))
        else if ...
```

Let's now look at the application of this algorithm to the expression *abx*, internally stored in the representation $(a \cdot b) \cdot x$. In the interests of readability we replace the hard to read $dif(f(x),x)$ with $(f(x))'$.

$$((a \cdot b) \cdot x)' =$$

$$((a \cdot b)' \cdot x) + ((a \cdot b) \cdot (x)') =$$

$$((((a)' \cdot b) + (a \cdot (b)')) \cdot x) + ((a \cdot b) \cdot 1) =$$

$$(((0 \cdot b) + (a \cdot 0)) \cdot x) + ((a \cdot b) \cdot 1)$$

The result of this symbolic differentiation is thus the rather bizarrely written expression $(0 \cdot b + a \cdot 0) \cdot x + (a \cdot b) \cdot 1$. Here the second part of the ›Simplify‹ comes into play, using the various algebraic identities to produce the more easily read equivalent expression $a \cdot b$.

Multiplying longer numbers

At school, one learns to multiply numbers as follows:

```
1234 × 5678
6170
 7404
  8638
   9872
7006652
```

In the process, every digit in the first number is multiplied with every digit in the second number. The computational complexity of this algorithm is n^2, where n is the length of the numbers to be multiplied, that is, the number of digits. (For simplicity we assume the numbers have the same length.) The complexity term for the addition is ignored because it does not contribute significantly, in comparison to the n^2 multiplications.

To multiply two thousand-digit numbers together, one requires one million computational steps. For ten thousand digit numbers, we need one hundred million. Doesn't it go faster than that?

Even though it seems hard to imagine, the algorithm *can* be accelerated! In computer algebra systems even improvements on such a low level are significant.

In the following the symbols x and y represent digit sequences (e.g. 1234 and 5678) while x' and y' the numbers that correspond to these digit sequences (e.g. 1234 and 5678).

With the assumption that the digit sequences x and y are both of length n, they can be treated as the upper sequences xo, yo and lower sequences xu, yu, where xo, xu, yo and yu are each composed of $n/2$ digits.

x	=	xo	xu

y	=	yo	yu

Obviously we can state

$$x' = xo' \cdot 10^{n/2} + xu', \quad y' = yo' \cdot 10^{n/2} + yu'$$

for the numbers corresponding to the sequences. For the product $x' \cdot y'$ we can readily see:

$$x' \cdot y' = (xo' \cdot 10^{n/2} + xu') \cdot (yo' \cdot 10^{n/2} + yu') =$$

$$= xo' \cdot yo' \cdot 10^{n} + (xo' \cdot yu' + xu' \cdot yo') \cdot 10^{n/2} + xu' \cdot yu'$$

A multiplication by a power of 10 does not affect the calculation time, since it is simply a shift operation. The work necessary for addition can also be ignored. Thus, using the last equivalence, we can see that the multiplication of two numbers of length n (namely $x' \cdot y'$) can be equivalently performed through four multiplications of numbers of length $n/2$ (namely $xo' \cdot yo'$, $xo' \cdot yu'$, $xu' \cdot yo'$ and $xu' \cdot yu'$).

The multiplication algorithm has nevertheless a computational complexity of n^2, since

$$4 \cdot (n/2)^2 = 4 \cdot (n^2/4) = n^2$$

thus no advantage. The following identity is however priceless:

$$(xo' \cdot yu' + xu' \cdot yo') = (xo' + xu') \cdot (yo' + yu') - xo' \cdot yo' - xu' \cdot yu'$$

Putting this into the expression above, one sees:

$$x' \cdot y' = xo' \cdot yo' \cdot 10^{n} + ((xo' + xu') \cdot (yo' + yu') - xo' \cdot yo' - xu' \cdot yu') \cdot 10^{n/2} + xu' \cdot yu'$$

In this formulation we have three multiplications of numbers of length $n/2$ on the right, since the two products $xo' \cdot yo'$ and $xu' \cdot yu'$ are used twice, and the numbers $xo' + xu'$ and $yo' + yu'$ have length at most $n/2 + 1$. From this observation Karatsuba and Ofman developed the following multiplication algorithm in 1962:

```
Algorithm '*'; Input: x,y; Output: z
    determine xo, xu, yo, yu
    zo:= xo * yo
    zu:= xu * yu
    zm:= (xo + xu) * (yo - yu) - zo - zu
    z:= zo × 10^n + zm × 10^(n/2) + zu
```

The reduction by halves is applied recursively. This algorithm has the computational complexity $n^{ld3} \approx n^{1.59}$. For the example above we see:

```
xo:=12; xu:=34; yo:=56; yu:=78
zo:=12*56=672
zu:=34*78=2652
zm:=(12+34)*(56+78)-672-2652=46*134-672-2652
z:= 672....
       2840..
         2652
     7006652
```

Of course the improvement appears only for larger numbers. For smaller numbers the administrative load of decomposition is more than the improvement in speed. The basis of this algorithm is also applicable to multiplication of polynomials.

Symbolic integration

To integrate the rather unwieldy expression

$$r(x):=\frac{3x^{11} - 2x^{10} + 7x^9 + 2x^7 + 23x^6 - 10x^5 + 18x^4 - 9x^3 + 8x^2 - 3x + 1}{3x^9 - 2x^8 + 7x^7 - 4x^6 + 5x^5 - 2x^4 + x^3},$$

one proceeds as follows:

❑ [A]uthor (3x^11-2x^10+7x^9+2x^7+.....) [↵]

   [C]alculus [I]ntegrate [↵] [↵] [↵]

```
         11      10      9      7       6       5       4      3      2
      3·x    - 2·x   + 7·x  + 2·x  + 23·x  - 10·x  + 18·x  - 9·x  + 8·x  - 3·x +
#1:  ──────────────────────────────────────────────────────────────────────────
              9      8      7      6      5      4      3
           3·x  - 2·x  + 7·x  - 4·x  + 5·x  - 2·x  + x

     ⌠      11      10      9      7       6       5       4      3      2
     ⎮   3·x    - 2·x   + 7·x  + 2·x  + 23·x  - 10·x  + 18·x  - 9·x  + 8·x  - 3·x
#2:  ⎮  ──────────────────────────────────────────────────────────────────────────
     ⌡         9      8      7      6      5      4      3
              3·x  - 2·x  + 7·x  - 4·x  + 5·x  - 2·x  + x
```

[S]implify [↵]

```
              ⎡ √2·(3·x - 1) ⎤                            2
     2·√2·ATAN ⎢ ──────────── ⎥                 2·LN(3·x  - 2·x + 1)      LN(x  + 1)
#3:  ─────────────────────────── + ATAN(x) +    ──────────────────── - ──────────
                 3                                       3                   2
```

The answer, much wider than the screen and therefore truncated, can be calculated on a 33-MHz-PC-486 in 1.4 seconds. How does a computer algebra system integrate? It turns out that integration, in comparison to differentiation, is a very complex task that cannot be completely described.

There exists an algorithm which for any elementary transcendental function $f(x)$

- decides if $\int f(x)dx$ is representable as an elementary transcendental function $g(x)$,
- and in the case that this is so, effectively computes $g(x)$.

It originates with Risch in 1969, but has never been completely implemented in any system. Implementation difficulties due to algorithmic details, as well as the large administrative load even for small examples, have conspired to keep all implementations partial. Thus in most systems a mixture of heuristics and efficient algorithms for special cases in implemented.

In the following we look at such a special case algorithm for the integration of rational functions. Parallel to the explanation of the algorithm we look at the example presented above.

We have a rational function $r(x) = \dfrac{u(x)}{v(x)}$, where u and v are polynomials. We are searching for a function s so that $s(x) = \int r(x)dx$.

Step 1: Bring $r(x) = \dfrac{u(x)}{v(x)}$ in the form $r(x) = p(x) + \dfrac{a(x)}{b(x)}$, where the order of the polynomial a is properly lower than the order of the polynomial b.

As an example we have:

$$p(x):= x^2$$
$$a(x):= 4x^8 - 3x^7 + 25x^6 - 11x^5 + 18x^4 - 9x^3 + 8x^2 - 3x + 1$$
$$b(x):= 3x^9 - 2x^8 + 7x^7 - 4x^6 + 5x^5 - 2x^4 + x^3$$

Step 2: Find a squarefree factorisation $b = b_1^{e_1} \cdot b_2^{e_2} \cdot \ldots \cdot b_k^{e_k}$ and then decompose
$$\frac{a(x)}{b(x)} = \sum_{i=1}^{k} \sum_{j=1}^{e_i} \frac{a_{i,j}(x)}{b_i^{\,j}(x)}.$$

For the example this means:

$$b(x) = (3x^2 - 2x + 1)(x^2 + 1)^2 x^3$$
$$\text{thus: } b_1(x):= 3x^2 - 2x + 1, \ b_2(x):= x^2 + 1, \ b_3(x):= x$$
$$\frac{a(x)}{b(x)} = \frac{4x}{3x^2 - 2x + 1} + \frac{-x}{x^2 + 1} + \frac{3x + 2}{(x^2 + 1)^2} + \frac{1}{x} + \frac{-1}{x^2} + \frac{1}{x^3}$$

Thus so far we have $\int r(x)dx = \int p(x)dx + \sum_{i=1}^{k}\sum_{j=1}^{e_i}\int \frac{a_{i,j}(x)}{b_i^{\ j}(x)}dx$. Since p is a

polynomial, it is simple to find $\int p(x)dx$, and all that remains is to compute the

integral $\int \frac{a_{i,j}(x)}{b_i^{\ j}(x)}dx$. (In the case that $b_l(x) = x$ for some $1 \le l \le k$, then the integrals

$\int \frac{a_{l,j}(x)}{b_l^{\ j}(x)}dx = \int \frac{a_{l,j}}{x^j}dx$ for $1 \le j \le e_l$ are easy to find.)

For the example this means:

$$\int r(x)dx =$$

$$= \frac{x^3}{3} + \int \frac{4x}{3x^2 - 2x + 1}dx + \int \frac{-x}{x^2 + 1}dx + \int \frac{3x + 2}{(x^2 + 1)^2}dx + \int \frac{1}{x}dx + \int \frac{-1}{x^2}dx + \int \frac{1}{x^3}dx =$$

$$= \frac{x^3}{3} + \int \frac{4x}{3x^2 - 2x + 1}dx + \int \frac{-x}{x^2 + 1}dx + \int \frac{3x + 2}{(x^2 + 1)^2}dx + \ln(x) + \frac{1}{x} - \frac{1}{2x^2}$$

Step 3: For every $j \ge 2$, reduce the integral $\int \frac{a_{i,j}(x)}{b_i^{\ j}(x)}dx$ to $\int \frac{\alpha_{i,j}(x)}{b_i^{\ j-1}(x)}dx$ using partial

integration until only denominators with exponent 1 remain.

In the example:

From $3x + 2 = 2 \cdot (x^2 + 1) + (-x + 3/2) \cdot (2x)$, we see

$$\int \frac{3x + 2}{(x^2 + 1)^2}dx = \int \frac{2}{x^2 + 1}dx + \int \frac{(-x + 3/2) \cdot (2x)}{(x^2 + 1)^2}dx =$$

$$= \int \frac{2}{x^2 + 1}dx + \frac{(-x + 3/2)(-1)}{x^2 + 1} - \int \frac{1}{x^2 + 1}dx =$$

$$= \frac{x - 3/2}{x^2 + 1} + \int \frac{1}{x^2 + 1}dx$$

and thus altogether:

$$\int r(x)dx =$$

$$= \frac{x^3}{3} + \int \frac{4x}{3x^2 - 2x + 1}dx + \int \frac{-x}{x^2 + 1}dx + \frac{x - 3/2}{x^2 + 1} + \int \frac{1}{x^2 + 1}dx + \ln(x) + \frac{1}{x} - \frac{1}{2x^2}$$

Step 4: For the remaining pieces $\int \frac{\alpha(x)}{\beta(x)}dx$ (for which we know that all β are

squarefree and $\deg\alpha < \deg\beta$) we c

$$\int \frac{\alpha(x)}{\beta(x)} dx = \sum_{i=1}^{n} c_i \cdot \ln(v_i), \text{ where}$$

- $c_1,\ldots,c_n$ are the zeroes of $\alpha(x) - c \cdot \beta'(x)$ and $\beta(x)$ and
- $v_i = \text{ggT}(\alpha(x) - c_i \cdot \beta'(x), \beta(x))$ for all $1 \le i \le n$.

In the example:

Rothstein's Theorem applied to $\int \dfrac{1}{x^2+1} dx$ gives:

$$\int \frac{1}{x^2+1} dx = \frac{i}{2}\ln(1-ix) - \frac{i}{2}\ln(1+ix) = \arctan(x)$$

The further applications of Rothstein's Theorem will be left as an exercise for the interested reader. Altogether we obtain:

$$\int r(x) dx =$$

$$\frac{x^3}{3} + \frac{2\sqrt{2}\arctan(\frac{\sqrt{2}(3x-1)}{2})}{3} + \frac{2\ln(3x^2 - 2x + 1)}{3} - \frac{\ln(x^2+1)}{2} + \frac{2x-3}{2(x^2+1)} + \arctan(x) + \ln(x) + \frac{1}{x} - \frac{1}{2x^2}$$

Simplification

It has been repeatedly stated in this and earlier chapters that simplification is a central activity and skill in mathematics, in particular in computer mathematics. Thus, and since the developers of computer algebra systems will not give access to their valuable secrets, we are prevented from discussing simplification.

The problems that arise through false simplification, the so-called over-simplifications, have already been referred to and discussed in Chapter 3. This current detour has been made only to introduce the following quote from Albert Einstein that the DERIVE developers made their central axiom:

"We should try to make things as simple as possible; but no simpler."

In this final chapter we use a thought accessory, namely a historical-philosophical panorama lens. It should help us to understand the meaning and influence of a tool such as DERIVE and thus understand a little bit more of the future. We start off back in the middle of the 18th century.

Around 1750 the steam engine was invented. With this tool, people could create power as and where needed from any flammable substances such as wood or coal. Both the ease of generation and the amount of power that could be generated made this a true quantum leap. The steam engine led to unimaginable possibilities: the industrial age had begun. Even today we are still amazed at what the steam engine and its logical successors (bulldozer, semitrailer, ocean liner, aeroplane, spaceship, etc.) can do.

Now we know that the potential of this invention is far outside what the people of the time could even begin to imagine. Their imaginations were of course limited by what they saw could be done with controllable power.

In the almost 250 years of the industrial age we have seen a large number of consequences, including:

❶ **Manual labour has become superfluous.** A competent trench digger will have trouble making a living from this skill today, because machines exist that can do the job faster, better and more cost effectively. Thus at the beginning of the industrial age, the basic manual skills began to be performed by machines instead of people. With the further development of machines it became possible to replace people performing more detailed and precise manual work. Industrial robots have made many trades redundant.

❷ **Survival of the strongest.** This was and is the basic paradigm of the industrial age. And strength was available through specific machines. In economic competition, the firm with better performing machinery had the advantage.

❸ **Physical exercise as recreation.** Before the industrial age, one *had* to use one's body to earn one's daily bread. Today that is no longer the case. However, most people realise that the body needs exercise so as not to fall into ruin. This is why so many people all over the world now take part in recreational sports such as jogging, aerobics, body-building and skiing in order to keep fit.

❹ **Physical Education becomes a school subject.** Schools have always had the task of giving an education for the mind. In our age, it is also necessary for students to learn that physical movement is necessary for their fitness and health. Thus Physical Education has been incorporated into the curriculum. The educator hopes that this understanding of the body will be carried into life after school.

❺ **Science and technical mathematics are introduced.** These subjects represent the sorts of knowledge that the industrial age has made possible. There are two reasons why these have become school subjects. On one hand, the students need a basic understanding of the machines that are an intrinsic part of our everyday lives. On the other hand, students are encouraged to become a part of the engineering system, to imagine or build their own machines. The system must at least be maintained. While mathematics was, from antiquity onwards, essentially an art form, in the industrial age it became a part of engineering science. The material taught in schools and universities has changed as a result, as we see by the inordinately tiny role that fundamental subjects such as Logic play in contemporary education.

❻ **Concentration on intellectual power.** People recognise that it is intellectual skills that differentiate them from machines, though it took several generations for this understanding to become widespread.

At this point in time (i.e. in these decades we are presently enjoying) we are in a phase of change. The industrial age is drawing to a close, leaving room for a new age.

In around 1950 the computer was invented. With this tool, people could create intellectual force (so to speak) as and when needed, at first principally in terms of memory and numerical calculation power. This invention caused a new quantum leap. With the computer, in particular with the possibilities of modern telecommunications, totally new possibilities arose: the Information Age had begun. When one looks at the multiplicity of products available today, from bookkeeping programs and flight simulators to mobile telephones and telebanking, one realises that we still do not know the boundaries of the potential that computers bring. The things that computers will make possible before the end of the Information Age are as unimaginable as space flight was in 1900.

When will that be? How long will the Information Age last? It is unlikely that it will be as long as 250 years, as all historical developments accelerate. It will probably be about one third as long, lasting around 70 or 80 years. If we draw a parallel between the Industrial Age and its effect on society, and the Information Age, it is clear that there are many changes still to come. For many of the ideas presented here there is no existent vocabulary, thus we have invented phrases that hopefully convey the ideas.

❶ **Intellectual labour becomes superfluous.** A competent bookkeeper would have a hard time earning a living from their skill today. Almost all firms use computers for such things. There are still people called bookkeepers, but their job is often reduced to data entry. At the beginning of the Information Age, the basic intellectual skills were taken over by machines. As computers develop, they take over finer skills. Mathematical skills such as differentiation, integration, simplification, etc. are examples of fine skills that will soon be as redundant as trench digging.

❷ **Survival of the better informed.** This is the new paradigm of the Information Age. Quick retrieval and dissemination of information and efficient digestion of relevant information are more important than productivity. In economic competition the firm that can best distribute information about its product has the advantage. Both the communication and the payment systems are becoming independent of physical media (Letter→Fax→Email, Cash→Credit-Cards→ Tele-banking) and only those firms that use these new media remain competitive. New methods of advertising (telemarketing, computer network advertising) become commonplace.

❸ **Intellectual training as recreation.** Up to the Information Age most people *had* to use their intellect. In the future fewer people will be required to, and will thus realise that the intellect needs to be exercised so as not to fall into ruin. "Thought Sports" may well become as popular in the twenty-first century as jogging is today. That this development is already happening is obvious from the sharply increasing sales figures of specialist books and (computer) games.

❹ **"Intellectual Education" is introduced as a school subject.** The maintenance of intellectual fitness will become a special part of the school system. What is currently mathematics offers itself as the possible content of such a course. (With this prognosis we make the recommendation that mathematics increases its compatibility with the Age of Information, so as not to be degraded to mere "Intellectual Education")

❺ **Computer science and problem-oriented mathematics become part of the curriculum.** These are the subjects that the Information Age has made possible. Incorporating them into the school curriculum serves two purposes. On one hand students should have a general understanding of the devices that are such a major part of their daily lives. On the other hand, students should be encouraged towards such professions as programmer or system designer, so development continues. Computer science is already being introduced, while problem oriented mathematics is where we see the future of what is currently known as mathematics. Mathematics has developed from an art to a form of engineering over the period of the Industrial Age. Now is the time for a further change, in part back to its roots, to problem-oriented mathematics.

❻ **Concentration on the creative powers.** People will realise that it is their creative powers that differentiate them from computers, though it will probably take several generations for this understanding to become widespread.

THE INDUSTRIAL AGE   1750

Manual Labour Becomes less Important.

Survival of the Fittest

Recreation:
Physical Fitness

School Health Focus:
Physical Education

School Subjects for System Maintenance:
Science, Technical Mathematics

Concentration On:
Intellectual Powers

1950   THE INFORMATION AGE

Intellectual Labour Becomes less Important

Survival of the Better-informed

Recreation:
Intellectual Fitness, "Thought Sport"

School Health:
Intellectual Education

School Subjects for System Maintenance:
Computer Science, Problem-Oriented Mathematics

Concentration on:
Creative Powers

When we speak here of physical, intellectual and creative skills, clearly any human skill is a balanced mixture of all three. Take the following examples:

- Follow this person.
- Go on this road from here to Place A.
- Go, with the guidance of this city map, from here to Place A.
- Go from here to Place A (i.e. without further information on the whereabouts of Place A).

In the first case it is almost only physical skills that are needed. Intellectual skills are only necessary insofar as to be prepared to follow the leader, and to do this. The use of one's creative skills in this task would be useless, or even damaging to the chances of carrying out the command. The second case is almost as physical as the first, though a little more intellectual skill is necessary. Creative skill remains as unnecessary as before. The third case is more of an intellectual task, the physical ability to move being taken for granted. Essentially the intellectual skills Reading-a-Map and Follow-a-Path-on-a-Map-Through-a-City are needed. For the fourth case the creativity becomes necessary, to imagine where to even obtain information about how to get to Place A.

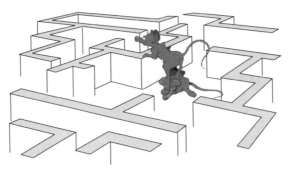

In this sense we need to go back over the previous statements about purely physical, intellectual and creative powers and to relativise them, combine them and otherwise make them more realistic. Nevertheless they do not lose their relevance or validity.

Contemporary mathematics in schools is somehow like portrait painting in the age of photography. The best artist in terms of working with mathematical symbols will have it as difficult in the future as the portrait painter of today.

What will come after the information age? Well, in the Industrial Age people concentrated on their intellectual powers and then, or perhaps therefore, developed a machine that could amplify this intellectual power. It could be that as we concentrate on our creative powers in this Information Age, we come to develop a machine that increases our creative powers. Thus the next age would be a Creative Age, starting shortly after the step into the next millennium, with the development of a Creativity Machine. Who knows?

But enough speculation. To finish we bring together the most important implications of this comparison. From the recognition and realisation of the similarities and differences between historical processes one can make prognoses and prepare for what seems probable. Therein lies the relevance of historical research and the application of the study of history.

- If mathematics remains as it is then the danger exists that it will be rationalised away to the level of Physical Education or Music today.
- In order to play a leading role, the teaching of mathematics must adapt itself to the needs and methods of the current age. Principally this means that we must make ourselves aware of the fundamental difference between machines and people; creativity. This must stand as the central pillar of mathematics in the future.
- With DERIVE, the teacher of mathematics has a tool in his/her hand that can help to make the changes needed for this new direction.

With this in mind: let's get down to it. The hour is at hand!

MATHEMATICAL BOOKS FROM CHARTWELL-BRATT

Backstrom, Gunnar
Fields of Physics on the PC by Finite Element Analysis

How physicists and engineers can use FEA (finite element analysis) to solve partial differential equations (PDEs) occurring in various fields of classical physics: gravity, electricity and magnetism, heat conduction, elastic deformation, and liquid flow.

£19.95 • 312 pp • 1994 • ISBN 0-86238-382-X

Backstrom, Gunnar
Practical Mathematics using MATLAB

The idea behind the present volume is to apply the main results of first-year university mathematics, starting with only a handful of MATLAB statements and gradually introducing more, as the need arises.

£14.95 • 1995 • ISBN 0-86238-397-8

Bartholomew-Biggs, M.
The Essentials of Numerical Computation

Introduction to some commonly-used numerical techniques for problems of curve fitting and approximation, integration, equation solving, differential equations, eigenvalue calculations and optimisation.

£8.95 • 241 pp • 1982 • ISBN 0-86238-029-4

Berry, J. Kronfellner, M. Kutzler, B. Monaghan, J. (eds)
Computer Algebra in Mathematics Education

The calculator changed the teaching of numerical mathematics forever. Now, low-cost computer algebra software, and the new Texas Instruments TI-92 calculator, are revolutionising teaching of advanced mathematics. As with any powerful tool, guidance in its use is necessary. This book is a collaboration between many of the world's leading experts on using computer algebra systems to teach mathematics. It distills their combined expertise into one volume and represents the state of the art.

£19.95 • 1996 • ISBN 0-86238-430-3

Berry, J. Graham, E. & Watkins, A. J.
Learning Mathematics through DERIVE

This book develops foundation mathematics for scientists and engineers through the use of DERIVE. It emphasises the role of DERIVE as an investigative tool to introduce and help students to understand basic concepts in mathematics and as a problem solving tool for solving real problems from the world of science and engineering. Written primarily for students who have not studied maths at A-level or equivalent, or who are entering a science or engineering degree at the foundation level. However the book will also provide an introduction to the use of DERIVE to those students who are already familiar with scientific functions and calculus. Contents: Introductory functions. Exponential and logarithmic functions. Trigonometric functions. Sequences and series. Simple numerical methods for solving equations. Differentiation. Integration. Numerical methods. Differential equations. Complex numbers. Matrices. Readership: Post-16 mathematics through to undergraduate level.

£15.95 • 370 pages • 1994

Burton, L. & Jaworski, B. (eds)

Technology in Mathematics Teaching - a bridge between teaching and learning

This book addresses issues raised by the introduction of technology into the teaching and learning of mathematics. It uses the metaphor of technology acting as a 'bridge' between the teacher's planning and the learner's developing understanding.

£19.95 • 496 pp • 1995 • ISBN 0-86238-401-X

Böhm, Josef

Teaching Mathematics with Derive

This illustrated guide is packed full of sound advice and teaching materials. Top European educationalists show how to use computer algebra systems to teach mathematics, particularly to 12-18 year olds.

£13.95 • 298 pp • 1993 • ISBN 0-86238-319-6

Denton, B.

Learning Linear Algebra through DERIVE

Using the computer algebra package DERIVE, this book reinforces theoretical knowledge while making applications more realistic. It can also be used with packages such as Macsyma, 'latlab, Maple and Mathematica requiring only a few adjustments. Numerous problems with solutions are provided to reinforce the theory. Independent learning is encouraged. Contents: Introduction to Matrices. Vectors with Applications to Geometry. Systems of Linear Equations. Vech spaces. Linear Transformation. Eigenvectors and eigenvalues. Conclusions. Solutions.

£16.95 • 296 pages • 1995

Easton, A. K. & Steiner, J. M.

The Role of Mathematics in Modern Engineering

Fascinating collection of papers on industrial applications mathematics, mathematical modelling in engineering, mathematical techniques for engineers, and mathematical education of engineers.

£50 • 724 pp • 1996 • ISBN 0-86238-421-4

Engquist, B. & Gustafsson, B.

Third International Conference on Hyperbolic Problems: theory, numerical methods and applications; Vols 1&2

£65.00 • 1991 • ISBN 0-86238-285-8

Etchells, T. Hunter, M. Monaghan, J. Pozzi, S. Rothery, A.

Mathematical Activities with Computer Algebra: a photocopiable resource book

This photocopiable resource book is the first of a new generation of support materials for the educational use of computer algebra. Designed to be used with any computer algebra system, the authors go beyond mere button pressing and show how to harness the power of computer algebra systems for educational purposes.

£20 • 116 pp • 1996 • ISBN 0-86238-405-2

Little, C. & Sutherland, R.
Geometry with Cabri - Exploring Trigonometry

This booklet presents ideas and activities for using Cabri-Géomètre to teach trigonometry. The activities may be photocopied.

£9 • 26 pp • 1995 • ISBN 0-86238-376-5

Little, C. & Sutherland, R.
Geometry with Cabri - Taking A New Angle

Presents ideas for using Cabri Géomètre school geometry software to explore elementary properties of angles at a point, between parallel lines and in triangles and polygons. The activities may be photocopied.

£9 • 20 pp • 1995 • ISBN 0-86238-377-3

Little, C. & Sutherland, R.
Geometry with Cabri - Transforming Transformations

Using Cabri-Géomètre school geometry software to analyse and explore the plane isometric transformations - reflection, translation, and rotation. The activities may be photocopied.

£9 • 34 pp • 1995 • ISBN 0-86238-378-1

McLaren, D.
Numerical Analysis and Spreadsheets

Using spreadsheets as a powerful tool to discover numerical analysis at college and undergraduate level. Basic methods for numerical integration, solution of linear and non-linear equations, and solution of ordinary and partial differential eqations.

approx £13.95 • 1996 • ISBN 0-86238-431-1

Persson Lars Erik, et al
The Homogenisation Method - an introduction

Problem- solving in mechanics and physics using this branch of applied mathematics.

£14.95 • 1993 • ISBN 0-86238-334-x

Rich, N. Rose, J. & Gilligan, L.
Mastering the TI-92: Explorations from Algebra through Calculus

The TI-92 calculator from Texas Instruments includes versions of DERIVE and Cabri Géomètre II in addition to the functionality of a TI-82. Part One of this book is an overview of virtually all the important features of the TI-92. It provides the reader with a certain level of comfort with the TI-92 as well as a continuing reference for the machine's features. Part Two takes the reader into the mathematics curriculum by applying the TI-92 in twelve Explorations. These explorations (or projects) are in the areas of algebra, geometry, precalculus, and calculus. Part Three highlights the programming features of the TI-92 and includes eleven programs of varying degrees of difficulty. One of the strengths of the book is that it provides over 600 screens of the TI-92's various applications. It also provides hundreds of examples demonstrating how to use the various keys, menus, and submenus.

£19.95 • 200 pp • 1996

Grevholm, B. & Hanna, G.
Gender and Mathematics Education

This book will be essential as a text in both graduate and undergraduate courses in mathematics education, psychology and sociology of education and women's studies.

£28 • 428 pp • 1995 • ISBN 0-86238-408-7

Heugl, H. & Kutzler, B.
DERIVE in Education - opportunities and strategies

Leading experts in the educational use of the DERIVE computer algebra system advise on its educational use at various academic levels. Equally applicable to use of the Texas Instruments TI-92 calculator, which contains a version of DERIVE.

£19.95 • 302 pp • 1994 • ISBN 0-86238-351-X

Hill, R. & Keagy, T.
Elementary Linear Algebra with DERIVE: an integrated text

In this text extensive use is made of the Derive symbolic computer software system to simplify calculations and allow the learner and user to focus on the beauty of the structure of linear algebra and its associated applications. To support the learner, the text includes 180 example problems worked in detail, almost 600 Derive statements illustrating the use of the computer software, and more than 600 exercises with the solutions to most included in an appendix.

£14.95 • 392 pp • 1995 • ISBN 0-86238-403-6

Kutzler, B.
Improving Mathematics Teaching with DERIVE

This is one of the most important books ever written on the subject of teaching mathematics. The world's leading expert on teaching mathematics with the popular DERIVE computer algebra system (also available on the Texas Instruments TI-92 calculator) shows how to use it in the classroom. Alternative implementation strategies are offered to suit different topics and situations. He also advises, convincingly, on how this new technology will change curricula and teaching methods. The book is full of clearly presented practical examples and is a must for every mathematics teacher.

£14.50 • 185 pp • 1996 • ISBN 0-86238-422-2

Kutzler, B.
✳ Mathematics on the PC: Introduction to DERIVE

An introduction to DERIVE software and its use in teaching mathematics at any level.

£14.50 • 164 pp • 1994 • ISBN n/a

Laflin, S.
Numerical Methods of Linear Algebra

Numerical methods for solving sets of linear equations and calculating the eigenvalues and eigenvectors of matrices are explored in theory and practice in this clearly written book.

£8.95 • 170 pp • 1989 • ISBN 0-86238-151-7

Rothery, A.
Modelling with Spreadsheets

The book explains and illustrates both the principles of modelling and the use of computer spreadsheet methods. The general reader, business spreadsheet user, teacher, school or college student will find it enjoyable and informative. It can be used with any spreadsheet. The author is one of the world's leading educationalists in this field.

£5.95 • 63 pp • 1990 • ISBN 0-86238-258-0

Råde, L.
Teaching of Modern Engineering Mathematics

Experiences of teachers worldwide. Based on the 4th European Seminar on Mathematics in Engineering Education.

£16.95 • 225 pp • 1988 • ISBN 0-86238-173-8

Råde, L. & Westergren, B.
Mathematics Handbook for Science and Engineering

The latest version of the most comprehensive mathematics reference book available for scientists, engineers and university students (previously entitled "Beta Mathematics Handbook"). As well as classical areas of maths such as algebra, geometry and analysis, it also covers areas of particular current interest : discrete mathematics, probability and statistics, programming and numerical statistics. It concentrates on definitions, results, formulas, graphs and tables, and emphasizes concepts and methods with applications in technology and science.

£18.00 • 539 pp • 1996 • ISBN 0-86238-406-0

Råde, Lennart
ALPHA-Mathematics Handbook

A useful and concise information source for basic areas of mathematics, numerical analysis, computer science, probability theory and statistics. Primarily intended for students at college level.

£9.95 • 199 pp • 1984 • ISBN 0-86238-036-7

Schagen, I.P.
Statistics and Operations Research

Introductory book with plenty of examples, exercises and projects. Based on a second year university course.

£8.95 • 300 pp • 1986 • ISBN 0-86238-077-4

Schumann, H. & Green, D.
Discovering Geometry with a Computer using Cabri Géométre

Provides a wide- ranging discussion of geometrical investigation aided by a computer. Although the book begins with an introduction to one particular software package - Cabri-Géométre - to which it refers throughout, most of the activities suggested will be of interest to users of other software packages such as Geometer's Sketchpad and Geometry Inventor.

£19.95 • 288 pp • 1995 • ISBN 0-86238-373-0

Sjöstrand, David
Mathematics with Excel

This new book aims to show how Excel can be used to visualise and understand mathematics. Intended for students at secondary school and college level, it contains many examples with detailed instructions and exercises. It can be used by students with little or no experience of spreadsheets, as well as by advanced Excel users. (Reprint with amendments.)

£13.95 • 190 pp • 1996 • ISBN 0-86238-361-7

Smith, Harry V.
Numerical Methods of Integration

This book describes, with the aid of worked examples and supplementary problems, many of the more recent and important techniques for the numerical evaluation of definite integrals. Extremely useful to undergraduate/postgraduate students, engineers, mathematicians and scientists; in fact, to anyone who has to approximate a definite integral.

£9.95 • 147 pp • 1993 • ISBN 0-86238-331-5

Soper, J, & Lee, M.
Statistics with Lotus 1-2-3: 2nd Edition

Shows how any spreadsheet, with particular emphasis on Lotus 123, can be used as a powerful statistical tool, for business or academic use. Readers will profit from applying spreadsheet analysis beyond the usual fields of budgeting and costing. The practical approach means that students in any discipline can use it in introductory statistics courses.

£9.95 • 224 pp • 1990 • ISBN 0-86238-244-0

Steiner, J.M.
Mathematics in Engineering

An Australian perspective on the role of mathematics in engineering and its relevance to industrial needs. Based on papers written by prominent members of the Australian Engineering Mathematics Group.

£21.00 • 192 pp • 1993 • ISBN 0-86238-318-8

van Tilborg, Henk C. A.
Error-Correcting Codes - a first course

Intended for students in mathematics, computing science, and those students in electrical engineering who major in information theory. The book constitutes a solid basis in error-correction techniques and provides an excellent start for further study. The level of the text is aimed at third or fourth year undergraduate students.

£25.00 • 235 pp • 1993 • ISBN 0-86238-338-2

Townend, S. & Pountney, D.

⋇⋇ **Learning Modelling with DERIVE**

Teaches mathematical modelling using the algebraic software package, DERIVE. Mathematical modelling is very much the fashion as the maths syllabus develops towards applications and problem solving.

Gently guides the reader through the problem formulating and solutions stages of modelling.

Provides a wide range assortment of case studies to illustrate issues.

Contents: Introduction. Geometric and Trigonometric Models. Algebraic Models. Optimisation-based Models. Calculus-based Models. Discrete Models. Differential Equations-based Models. Statistical & Simulations Models. The Techniques of Dimensional Analysis.

£15.95 • 256 pages • 1995

Wan, Zhe-xian

Geometry of Classical Groups over Finite Fields

A good reference for those who work on classical groups, finite fields, finite geometry, combinatorics, block designs and coding theory. Only basic knowledge of abstract and linear algebra is required.

£29.95 • 394 pp • 1993 • ISBN 0-86238-326-9

Wan, Zhe-xian

Introduction to Abstract and Linear Algebra

A solid algebraic base for those who wish to become specialists in, e.g., coding theory, cryptography, and linear systems theory.

£29.95 • 369 pp • 1992 • ISBN 0-86238-316-1

Watkins, A.J.P.

DERIVE-based Investigations for Post-16 Core Mathematics

Practical investigations using the DERIVE computer algebra system or Texas Instruments TI-92 calculator to explore advanced maths.

£9.95 • 102 pp • 1993 • ISBN 0-86238-312-9